The following are the files needed to create the website and DOD-JavaScript-Handbook; How To Code JavaScript without Tools. Create a training folder in your Documents folder called DOD-JSHB. Copy and paste each HTML page into a blank page begining with <!DOCTYPE html> and ending with </html> . Save (save as) each HTML document with MSNotepad application with corresponding name. The document type (Save as type) needs to change to ALL Files before adding the name and saving the file in the folder. Default document type is .txt and will be added automatically unless you specify ALL Files.

HTML document must end in .html to be viewable via a browser application.
****

Lindex.html
****

```
<!DOCTYPE html>
<html lang="en">
<head>
<meta charset="utf-8">
<title>JS DOD-HB Page 0-0</title>
<style>//css goes here </style>
<SCRIPT LANGUAGE="JavaScript">
// JavaScript functions go here or in body
</SCRIPT>
</head>
<body>
<center>
<h3>(JS) JavaScript DOD HandBook</h3><br>
<h4>How to code without coding tools Page 0 </h4><br>
</center>
<p><blockquote>
```

So why learn JavaScript or coding at all. All civilian and military employed by the military become more valuable as an asset as they develope skills and experience. For many getting a retirement for 20 years of youthful service they plan on moving into the commercial world or as a federal civilian. <i>JavaScript is the fastest growing programming language.</i> All major commercial companies use it; Google, Facebook, Amazon and host of others. It is used primarily to interact with a customer or user and check accuracy of user inputs. This is why it was invented to test user inputs. So when you click on a button or enter some information it is likely JavaScript doing that on a webpage. JavaScript is the dominant client-side scripting language of the Web, with 98% of all websites (mid–2022) using it for this purpose. Scripts are embedded in or included from HTML documents and interact with the DOM (Document Object Model). More on DOM later but you can interact, add, change, adjust any portion of the webpage inside JavaScript "on the fly". DOM is a loaded "object" of every tag, attribute, and element of a HTML webpage. All major web browsers have a built-in JavaScript interpetive engine that executes the code on the user's device eliminating webserver overhead.

JavaScript civilian Federal programmers earn about $72000 dollars a year even within the DOD. Author was paid DOD programmer for over 10 years. This skill is perhaps one of the most sought after skills to assist in IT data field. These skilled programmers are needed to

develope front end web sites and back end database sites. Experienced professional are the players in full stack websites. The most basic skill needed in the any web workplace. Including cell phone apps that interact with databases.

So where to begin. All journeys start out at a beginning point. In programming that point is learning the language. Much like learning a different verbal language say Spanish for an English speaking person. You start with the basic sounds and appearance of the the letters used in the language. Usually use an "interpeter" or translator until you become familiar with the language. Programming is talking computer talk to a computer. Because we do not talk in eight groups of zeros and ones, 00111111, common to computers we need an interperter to talk to the computer. The program language lets us talk english and the interperter talks computer to the computer. This JavaScript interperter or translator has been loaded into every internet browser as a "defacto" standard since the beginning (1995).(Defacto standards is applied or adopted by creators of different browsers to remain competitive so everyone installed it). It has become more powerful as it developed with the industry development.

So a computer (Igor) is a data servant or slave if you will. You tell (Igor) "get me data" and (Igor) answers, "yes master". If you speak english it replies 00111111 which is equal to ? in (Igor's language) with puzzled expression. "Huh?", Igor is not stupid he or she did not understand what you said.

Because of security concerns DOD and many larger commercial companies have limited some of standard tools for day to day use. Like a forklift operator at Amazon would not have access to the coding tools normally. The hackers learned early they could copy the source code of a webpage then misdirect a unsuspecting user to their site to collect critical privacy and financial information. To counter this hacking many large companies and governments have turned off the ability to see the source code. Specifically <i>Professional Tools</i> is turned off in <i>each of the browsers</i> installed. Developement of coding is reserved to specific individuals with the "rights" to learn code. Professional Tools enable diagnostics and corrections in code and network traffic. One of the most important parts of the tools is the ability to view the actual <i>source code</i> behind the scenes of the webpages. The actual JavaScript language and executable coding called statements or commands are within the source code. This runs in the background to the user on a webpage. Also the error codes generated by the interpeter is turned off.

 Does this mean you can't create code? No it means the tools used to do that is not available generally. Also the rights to download and use commonly used commercial coding software is prohibited to most users. But for 15 years before Profession Tools were provided the source code was viewable in any text editor program or application. All that you need is a text editor and <i>knowledge of the language</i> to create web pages to run from your computer. You can learn "Vanilla JavaScript" or just "Plain JavaScript".

You can start with a simple text editor such as Microsoft Windows Notepad. With this editor you can view the source code.
 I will show you a simple way to learn the language and become good with it with MSNotepad. Then if you get a job to "code" you can do so with confidence and ease when the tools are provided. Besides it is fun to let your "inner" creative beast out and build something. So you use MSNotepad to view the source code of the HTML page and the associated JavaScript in the script tags. You "Display" this code on a html page with a browser. Okay let us begin with like a mini-course that will get you familiar with the code. In these examples I have made a barebones html page with and explaination of what is in the script tags and left out all the fluff of HTML and CSS that is often included. Then we will return after this

barebones course to a little more advanced scripting to assist you. Including a bunch of examples in real scenerios and games. BareBones JavaScript 10 sequential Pages <a href="barebones.html">JavaScript mini-bootcamp and Basics Page</a>
Menu and website links disabled on this page please visit the Basics Page.</p>
<!---<p>   Menu Page <a href="Lsite_menu.html"> Site Directory</a>   Begining Page <a href="Lindex.html">Start page</a>   Previous Page <a href="Lindex.html"> 1st page as you begin</a>   and Next Page <a href="pageL1.html">Next page</a></p> -->
<p style="color:lightgray">
Public Domain copywrite © version 0 - Author retains rights to any additional versions or editions
Author: Brent Lichfield
</p>
</body>
</html>
****

barebones.html
****

<!DOCTYPE html>
<html lang="en">
<head>
<title>
BareBones HTML-JavaScript
</title>
</head>
<body>
<h3>Mini-bootcamp BareBones Javascript</h3>
<p>This is a barebones HTML-JavaScript tutorial.
Purpose is to create a quick series of introductory lessons on the basics of JavaScript and how it works.
Introduce you to simple syntax of the language by showing you visually.
JavaScript is not Java language. OR an advanced complied language using a compiler usually on the webserver.
JavaScript is a browser interpetive language that is installed in the browser application within a user's PC.
Known as a client-side, this is the personal computer (PC) and uses only the memory, central processor,
and resources of the client.
JavaScript creates interactivity with the user and a HTML page displayed in a browser. Designed to verify
user input JavaScript does all the work on the user PC and does not use the internet or a server in the interaction.
</p>

<p>Okay some ground rules: Rule ONE anything contained in the script tags <script>// Javascript Code goes here</script>
MUST BE HANDTYPED! This forces you to learn to type the code and recognize when you have made a mistake.
Mistakes show up as blocks or lines of code that do not show up on the webpage. When you expect to see a result
and nothing shows up well then you need to check carefully the syntax (how it is written) one missing comma, semi-colon, extra space,
or quote can cause it.
 Rule Two pay attention to the details or refer to rule one.
 Rule three create necessary links
to move to next page.
 Rule 4 DO NOT skip the Exercises. Progressive built one then add scripts to it. </p>

<p>A <b>browser displays</b> html pages to the user of the PC. A html page is a any file with an extension of .html.
And you can create one by saving a file (save as) with nothing in it (empty) with a name like no-name.html via <b>MSNotepad</b> to view code.

Exercise 1: create no-name.html and view. (note to the wise student - must change the file extention file type to all files).
Exercise 2: create a start.html with the following html tags within it. AND create a index.html file with following html tags within it.
Exercise 3: change the title of each start page and index page to reflect what page they are. Save (not save as) and view
Exercise 4: change "Stuff to Display to the user goes here" to reflect start page or index page. Save (not save as) and view
Exercise 5: add Barebones lesson 1<a href="barebones1.html">Lesson1 Statements and Comments</a> to index.html
Just above the </body> tag

A barebones html has the following generally.

      <!DOCTYPE html>
      <html lang="en">
      <head>
      <title>BareBones_Template</title>
      <style>//CSS goes here</style>
      </head>
      <body>
      Stuff to Display to the user goes here

      <<b>script>// Body Javascript Code goes here</script></b>
      </body>
      </html>

All of these pages of the mini-bootcamp were created with MSNotepad and knowledge of the language.
You can create a webpage by just selecting and coping the code and give it a name with .html extension.

So to <b>see the code</b> you need to view the .html file in <b>MSNotepad</b> but to see the <b> results</b> in the webpage
You need to open the file using a <b>browser. Applications like Chrome or Bing</b>.
A Website is a collection of LINKED HTML pages.
</p>
<p>
Now off to lesson 1 <a href="barebones1.html">Lesson1 Statements and Comments</a>
</p>
<p style="color:lightgray">
Reference: https://www.youtube.com/watch?v=Ukg_U3CnJWl - Jake Wright - 2015
Public Domain copywrite version 0 - Author retains rights to any additional versions or editions
Author: Brent Lichfield
</p>
</body>
</html>

****
barebones1.html
****
<!DOCTYPE html>
<html lang="en">
<head>
<title>
BareBones1
</title>
</head>

<body>
<h3>Mini-bootcamp BareBones Javascript</h3>
<h3>Single Line Commands and Comments</h3>
<p>Okay within the barebones html file locate the <script>// Body Javascript goes here</script>
I write the following inside these tags. document.write("Hello World!");
like below.

<i><script><b>document.write("Hello World!");</b></script></i>

This is called a "<b>statement</b>" it is a command in JavaScript that is interpeted to the computer (PC) in machine
language and executed as a display to the browser screen. Whew! Means I printed "Hello World" on html page.
</p>

<script>document.write("<b>Hello World!</b>");</script>

<p><i><script><b>// this is a comment it goes here</b></script></i>

You can add comments like // this is a statement inside the script tags -single line comment
or /* add a paragraph or page of information */ it is not seen on the webpage but helps document
when, why or what for; when a coder is reviewing the code years later.

<i><script>// <b> Snippets </b> of code are the set of code statements that produce an output</script></i>

Snippets are useful as you can reuse that code in other projects later when creating something.

Exercise : create a snippets.html file from a start.html (save as)
Exercise : create a snip.js file (remember to save as and file type = All files)
Exercise : copy the italicized scripts and paste them in snippets.html in the body section of the HTML file
Exercise : view the scripts in snippets.html via a browser and MSNotepad
Exercise : hand write the scripts, the italicized scripts in snip.js then save.
</p>
<p>
Now off to lesson 2 <a href="barebones2.html">Lesson 2 - Variables</a>
</p>
<p style="color:lightgray">
Reference: https://www.youtube.com/watch?v=Ukg_U3CnJWI - Jake Wright - 2015
Public Domain copywrite version 0 - Author retains rights to any additional versions or editions
Author: Brent Lichfield
</p>
</body>
</html>
****
barebones2.html
****
<!DOCTYPE html>
<html lang="en">
<head>
<title>
BareBones2
</title>
</head>
<body>
<h3>Mini-bootcamp BareBones Javascript</h3>
<h3>Variables</h3>
<p>A <b>Variable</b> is "<i>data</i>" that has a name and a value. The name is the storage location within the PC RAM

random access memory. When JavaScript wants to retrieve that data value it does so by getting it from
the storage location by <i>name</i>. Some programing languages require you declare what type of data
you will be using. But JavaScript has primative types as default and does not need that done.
We create variables by using the <u>keyword</u> "var" then a name to the variable myVariable;
Using a var myVariable; will create a empty variable and becomes just a declaration of myVariable.
At this time myVariable is equal to <i>undefined</i>. To define it we can type myVariable = 5; or = "tom"; or whatever
definition we want via a = equal to something followed by a semi-colon.
Semi-colon is how interpter knows this is a JavaScript statement or command within the script tags.
Or we can shorten the definition by putting it all on one line like var myVariable = 5;
<script> var myVariable = 5; </script> this is the syntax of how to create a variable.
Generally strings like "tom" is done with quotation marks around it. Numbers declared is without quotations.
Tom without quotations is converted to a number by newer versions of JavaScript but in Vanilla or Plain JavaScript
might not be recognized so might not execute or run the statement at all.
And boolean type is a declared as either = true or = false. Useful in conditional testing discussed later.
Good practice is to provide comments like shown before with // comments about the variable.
View the following code and result below:

<i><script>
var newline = "<br>";
var mess1 = "myVariable is now ";
var mess2 = "Changed myVariable to ";
var myVar = 5;
document.write(mess1);
document.write(newline);
document.write(myVar); // result = 5
document.write(newline);
document.write(mess2);
var myVar = "tom";
document.write(myVar); // result = tom
document.write(newline);
document.write(mess2);
var myVar = true;
document.write(myVar); // result = true

document.write(newline);
document.write(mess2);
var myVar = "tom";
document.write(myVar); // result reset to tom
document.write(newline);
var myVar = 5;
document.write(mess1);
document.write(myVar); // result reset to 5
document.write(newline);
</script></i>

Running the above script results below.
</p>
<script>
var newline = "<br>";
var mess1 = "myVariable is now ";
var mess2 = "Changed myVariable to ";
var myVar = 5;
document.write(mess1);
document.write(newline);
document.write(myVar);
document.write(newline);
document.write(mess2);
var myVar = "tom";
document.write(myVar);
document.write(newline);
document.write(mess2);
var myVar = true;
document.write(myVar);
document.write(newline);
document.write(mess2);
var myVar = "tom";
document.write(myVar);
document.write(newline);
var myVar = 5;
document.write(mess1);
document.write(myVar);
document.write(newline);
</script>
Exercise: Write by hand the above scripts into snippets.html and view in browser
Exercise: Copy and paste the scripts into snip.js
<p>
Now off to lesson 3 <a href="barebones3.html">Lesson 3 - Operators & Math</a>
</p>
<p style="color:lightgray">

Reference: https://www.youtube.com/watch?v=Ukg_U3CnJWI - Jake Wright - 2015
Public Domain copywrite version 0 - Author retains rights to any additional versions or editions
Author: Brent Lichfield
</p>
</body>
</html>

****
barebones3.html
****

```
<!DOCTYPE html>
<html lang="en">
<head>
<title>
BareBones3
</title>
</head>
<body>
<h3>Mini-bootcamp BareBones Javascript</h3>
<h3>Operators and Math</h3>
<p>
```
The first operator is concate meaning to combine strings, we will create three variables
<i><script>
var words = "this is";
var morewords = " a sentence";
var newsentence = words + morewords; //plus sign combines or joins the variables
document.write (newsentence);
</script></i>
Running the script above, results are:
</p>
<script>
var words = "this is";
var morewords = " a sentence";
var newsentence = words + morewords;
document.write (newsentence);
</script>
<p> So we see that the var newsentence is a combination of words plus morewords
<i><script> var words = "this is";
var morewords = " a sentence";
var newsentence = words + morewords;
document.write (newsentence); </script></i>
We can also strip or substring the variable using var newsubstring = words(2,6); would yield "is is".

```
<i>Explained later with more details.</i><br>
</p>
<p>
We can use the plus sign in math instead of concate; it will add the values of the variables
together is numbers.<br>
<i>&lt;script&gt; <br>
var num1 = 5; <br>
var num2 = 3;<br>
var total = num1 + num2;<br>
document.write (total);<br>
Addition: var total = num1 + num2; using the + plus sign<br>
Other math actions you can do is
Subtraction: var total = num1 - num2; using the - negative sign<br>
Multiplication: var total = num1 * num2; using the * sign<br>
Division: var total = num1 - num2; using the / negative sign<br>
Remainder: var total = num1 % num2; using the % percent sign gives remainder of division<br>
&lt;/script&gt;</i><br>
Running the script above, results are shown below, also note that this another script in the html
page<br>
you can have as many as you like or need. Useful when performing functions more about that
later.<br>
</p>
<script>
var num1 = 5;
var num2 = 3;
var total = num1 + num2;
var add = "Addition <br>";
var newline = "<br>";
document.write (add);
document.write (total);
document.write (newline);
var sub = "Subtraction:";
var total = num1 - num2;
document.write (sub);
document.write (newline);
document.write (total);
document.write (newline);
var multi = "Multiplication";
var total = num1 * num2;
document.write (multi);
document.write (newline);
document.write (total);
document.write (newline);
var divide = "Division:";
```

```
var total = num1 / num2;
document.write (divide);
document.write (newline);
document.write (total);
document.write (newline);
var divideby = "Remainder:";
var total = num1 % num2;
document.write (divideby);
document.write (newline);
document.write (total);
document.write (newline);
</script>
<p>
```
There are some operators that take only one binary operator. Like the ++ plus,plus.
The plus plus will add one to the variable value say var num3 = 0; the ++num3; = 1
Would add one to 0 making it 1 and the if you put it after the variable like num3++ = 0
It would add one after that variable has displayed. The negative sign works similarly.
The capability is important in control loops. Discussed later.
<script>
var num3 = 0;
var num1 = 5;
var num2 = 3;
var total = ++num3 ;
var inc = "Incrementing
";
var newline = "<br>";
document.write (inc);
document.write (total);
document.write (newline);
</script>
Running the new script below.
</p>

```
<script>
var num3 = 0;
var num1 = 5;
var num2 = 3;
var total = ++num3;
var inc = "Incrementing<br>";
var newline = "<br>";
document.write (inc);
document.write (total);
document.write (newline);
</script>
```

Exercise: Write by hand the above italicized scripts into snippets.html and view in browser
Exercise: Copy and paste the scripts into snip.js

```
<p>
Now off to lesson 4 <a href="barebones4.html">Lesson 4 - Strings, & Arrays</a>
</p>
<p style="color:lightgray">
Reference: https://www.youtube.com/watch?v=Ukg_U3CnJWI - Jake Wright - 2015<br>
Public Domain copywrite version 0 - Author retains rights to any additional versions or
editions<br>
Author: Brent Lichfield
</p>
</body>
</html>
```

****

barebones4.html
****

```
<!DOCTYPE html>
<html lang="en">
<head>
<title>
BareBones4
</title>
</head>
<body>
<h3>Mini-bootcamp BareBones Javascript</h3>
<h3>Strings and Arrays</h3>
<p>
<u>Strings</u> are actually characters or words and stored as <u>Objects</u>. Meaning they
have a lot of hidden properties.<br> Objects can have many properties and values (attributes)
tied to each property. The hidden values take advanced coding.<br>
Strings internal properties includes <b>length() and substring() </b>. These are accessed by
variable name <br>
"." or dot length or "." dot substring like this var length = alpha.length for variable
alpha="abcdefg";<br>
length will return the number of characters in the variable value in this case it will be 7.<br>
Substring(x,y) takes two inputs, 1st character to start the count, and 2nd character to end the
count<br>
like var newalpha = alpha.substring(2,6); would give you cdef as a result. (Begin with 0).<br>
This is known as a "<b>Method</b>" meaning it takes and calculates a result based on a
property. <br>
<br> Code in the script tags:<br>
<i>&lt;script&gt;  <br>
var newline = "&lt;br&gt;"; <br>
var alength = "Length of the variable value";<br>
var alpha = "ABCDEFG";<br>
```

var length = alpha.length;
document.write(alength);
document.write(newline);
document.write(length);
document.write(newline);
var newalpha = alpha.substring(2,6);
document.write(alpha);
document.write(newline);
document.write(newalpha);
document.write(newline);
</script></i>
Yields the following:
</p>
<script>
var newline = "<br>";
var alength = "Length of the variable value";
var alpha = "ABCDEFG";
var length = alpha.length;
document.write(alength);
document.write(newline);
document.write(length);
document.write(newline);
var newalpha = alpha.substring(2,6);
document.write(alpha);
document.write(newline);
document.write(newalpha);
document.write(newline);
</script>
<p>
Arrays are special objects in they hold many different values within a single variable. Very useful if you want
to perform the same action or method against many values within the array. We create arrays using
the <b>new</b><u>Keyword</u> Array(7);. this will create a new array with 7 items in the array.
to add values to the array we use square brackets [ ] and we add the position inside the brackets
like
<i><script>
var array new Array(7);
a[0] = "Bear"; (first position begins with zero).
a[1] = "Elk"; (next first position from zero).
a[2] = "Bobcat"; (third value from beginning).
a[3] = "Mountain Lion"; (first position begins with zero).

a[4] = 90; (note you can enter numbers).
a[5] = "deer"; (if you fail to use quotes the string will be converted to a number and fail to run).
a[6] = true; (boolean words true and false or reserved as special value).
document.write(newline);
document.write(a[0] + coma +a[1] + coma +a[2] + coma +a[3] + coma +a[4] + coma +a[5] + coma +a[6]);
</script></i>
See how we can mix variable values and test against the various values if we wish.
</p>
<script>
var newline = "<br>";
var coma = ", ";
var arr = "Array has the following ";
var a = new Array(7);
a[0] = "Bear"; //(first position begins with zero).
a[1] = "Elk"; // (next first position from zero).
a[2] = "Bobcat"; //(third value from beginning).
a[3] = "Mountain Lion"; // (first position begins with zero).
a[4] = 90; // (note you can enter numbers).
a[5] = "deer";// (if you fail to use quotes the string will be converted to a number).
a[6] = true; //(boolean words true and false or reserved as special value).
document.write(arr);
document.write(newline);
document.write(a[0] + coma +a[1] + coma +a[2] + coma +a[3] + coma +a[4] + coma +a[5] + coma +a[6]);
</script>
<p>
Arrays can also be built using the following var b = new Array ("Moose", "Grouse", true, 20);
And they also can be built not using new key word like this var c = ["Antelop", "Buffalo", false, 17];
Outputing to the webpage is done the same by document.write(c[1]); would give you Buffalo.
</p>
Exercise: Write by hand the above italicized scripts into snippets.html and view in browser
Exercise: Copy and paste the scripts into snip.js
<p>
Now off to lesson 5 <a href="barebones5.html">Lesson 5 - Functions</a>
</p>
<p style="color:lightgray">
Reference: https://www.youtube.com/watch?v=Ukg_U3CnJWI - Jake Wright - 2015
Public Domain copywrite version 0 - Author retains rights to any additional versions or editions
Author: Brent Lichfield

```
</p>
</body>
</html>
```

****
barebones5.html
****

```
<!DOCTYPE html>
<html lang="en">
<head>
<title>
BareBones5
</title>
</head>
<body>
<h3>Mini-bootcamp BareBones Javascript</h3>
<h3>Functions</h3>
<p>
Functions are reuseable code, used or called, any where as many times as you would like.
These are built <br>
by using function keyword name of the <b>function() using curly brackets { //code;   } </b>like
this  <br>
<i>&lt;script&gt;  <br>
function sayHello(){ <br>
document.write("Hello Pioneer"); <br>
} <br>
&lt;/script&gt; </i> <br>
For example:<br><br>
<script>
function sayHello(){
document.write("Hello Pioneer");
}
sayHello();
var newline = "<br>";
document.write(newline);
</script><br><br>
We can call or <i>invoke</i> this function by entering sayHello(); in  the script tags.  Or create a
<i>trigger event</i><br>
within the HTML page to call the function "on click" in a form.<br>
We can also declare a variable within the function then give that variable a value when we call
the function.<br>
like <br>
<i>&lt;script&gt;  <br>
function sayHay(who){ <br>
```

```
document.write("Hello Pilgrim" + who); <br>
} <br>

sayHay("Tage");
&lt;/script&gt; </i> <br>
<script>
function sayHay(who){
document.write("Hello Pilgrim" + who);
}
sayHay("Tage");
</script>  <br>
</p>
Plus we can change the who input like sayHay("alice"); and the hello message.<br>
<script>
function sayHey(who){
document.write("Hello Padowan " + who);
}
sayHey("Tage");
var newline = "<br>";
document.write(newline);
sayHey("Alice");
var newline = "<br>";
document.write(newline);
</script>
<i>&lt;script&gt;<br>
function sayHey(who){ <br>
document.write("Hello Padowan " + who); <br>
}  <br>
sayHey("Tage");<br>
var newline = "&lt;br&gt;";<br>
document.write(newline);<br>
sayHey("Alice");<br>
var newline = "&lt;br&gt;";<br>
document.write(newline);<br>
&lt;script&gt;</i><br>
<br>
Exercise: Write by hand the above italicized scripts into snippets.html and view in browser<br>
Exercise: Copy and paste the scripts into snip.js<br>

<p>
Now off to lesson 6 <a href="barebones6.html">Lesson 6 - Control flow & Conditions
statements</a>
</p>
<p style="color:lightgray">
```

Reference: https://www.youtube.com/watch?v=Ukg_U3CnJWI - Jake Wright - 2015
Public Domain copywrite version 0 - Author retains rights to any additional versions or editions
Author: Brent Lichfield
</p>
</body>
</html>

****

barebones6.html
****

<!DOCTYPE html>
<html lang="en">
<head>
<title>
BareBones6
</title>
</head>
<body>
<h3>Mini-bootcamp BareBones Javascript</h3>
<h3>Flow Control and Conditional Statements</h3>
<p> If statements will only execute or run the code if a condition is true.
If we create a variable a =7;
<i><script>
if (a > 7){
// execute the following lines of code
}
</script> </i>
I will add an alert box asking user to click OKAY.
<i><script>
if (a > 7){
// execute the following lines of code
alert(a); // creates a pop up box for user to acknowledge by clicking
}
</script></i>
As you can see above a = 7 but not greater than 7 so no alert box will show up.
But if we change the value of the variable a = 12. A popup box asks for user to click OK.
</p>
<script>
var a = 12;
if (a > 7){
// execute the following lines of code
alert(a);
}

</script>
<p>
var a = 12;
if (a > 7){
// execute the following lines of code
alert(a); // creates a pop up box for user to acknowledge by clicking
}
We tested only if a > 7, a is greater than 7, we could have tested if a < 7, a is less than 7
or a => 7 equal to or greater than 7, a <= 7 a is equal to or less than 7
or a == 7 a is exactly equal to 7 or a === 7 a is exactly equal to 7 AND a number type not a character
or a != 7 a is NOT equal to 7 or any of the other tests above using ! in front.
</p>
<script>
var a = "jake";
if (a == "Jake"){
// execute the following lines of code
alert(a);
}

</script>
We can also test Strings. String of "jake" or 'jake' will see if they are exactly equal to Jake.
JavaScript is case sensitive so jake and Jake are NOT the same.
<i><script>
var a = "jake";
if (a == "Jake"){
// execute the following lines of code
alert(a);
}
</script> </i>
But if we change a = "Billie" and a == "Billie" are the same so the if statement will execute.
<script>
var a = "Billie";
if (a == "Billie"){
// execute the following lines of code
alert(a);
}

</script>
You can add a else {   } statement to test if the condition is false or a series of else statements.

<script>
var a = "jake";

```
if (a == "Jake"){
// execute the following lines of code
alert(a);
} else {
alert("The condition was false");
}

</script>
<i>&lt;script&gt;<br>
var a = "jake";<br>
if (a == "Jake"){<br>
// execute the following lines of code<br>
alert(a); <br>
} else {<br>
alert("The condition was false");<br>
}<br>

&lt;/script&gt;</i><br><br>

Exercise: Write by hand the above italicized scripts into snippets.html and view in browser<br>
Exercise: Copy and paste the scripts into snip.js<br>




<p>
Now off to lesson 7 <a href="barebones7.html">Lesson 7 - Loops</a>
</p>
<p style="color:lightgray">
Reference: https://www.youtube.com/watch?v=Ukg_U3CnJWI - Jake Wright - 2015<br>
Public Domain copywrite version 0 - Author retains rights to any additional versions or
editions<br>
Author: Brent Lichfield
</p>
</body>
</html>

******************************
barebones7.html
******************************

<!DOCTYPE html>
<html lang="en">
<head>
<title>
```

BareBones7
</title>
</head>
<body>
<h3>Mini-bootcamp BareBones Javascript</h3>
<h3>Loops</h3>
<p> There are many loops in JavaScript but the most useful one is a "for" loop, for (i =0; i<5; i++){ // code to execute }
i is a incremental variable we use as a counter, we are going to test if under 5, (loop) through code block until 5, then we will increment plus one to the counter.
Notice that the i variable was declared, given a value of zero, followed by a semicolon. Then the script will loop through the code block until
4 is reached and then after writing to the HTML page it will add one to the i variable. Forcing the loop to stop i > 4. Following in the script tags.
<i><script>
for (i =0; i<5; i++){
document.write("This is interating variable i " + i + "<br&gt");
// code to be executed
}
</script></i>
</p>
<script>
for (i =0; i<5; i++){
// code to be executed
document.write("This is interating variable i " + i + "<br>");
}
</script>

Exercise: Write by hand the above italicized scripts into snippets.html and view in browser
Exercise: Copy and paste the scripts into snip.js
<p>
Now off to lesson 8 <a href="barebones8.html">Objects</a>
</p>
<p style="color:lightgray">
Reference: https://www.youtube.com/watch?v=Ukg_U3CnJWI - Jake Wright - 2015
Public Domain copywrite version 0 - Author retains rights to any additional versions or editions
Author: Brent Lichfield
</p>
</body>
</html>

```
******************************
barebones8.html
******************************
<!DOCTYPE html>
<html lang="en">
<head>
<title>
BareBones8
</title>
</head>
<body>
<h3>Mini-bootcamp BareBones Javascript</h3>
<h3>Objects</h3>
```
Objects is data stored with one keyword or name but many properties (values) associated with that name. For instance a car is an object.
A car has many properties associated with it like the manufacture name, model, color, & how big the engine is.
The key_name = value does that look like a variable? Where as variables are single instance of name = value; objects are one name: but many values.

There are three ways to declare or create a object.
1st using the objectName={objectName:valueofname1, objectName:valueofname2, objectName:valueofname3} syntax
like a car={car.name:Dodge, car.model:Charger, car.color:White, car.motor:350Hemi} to get this car to do something
we will use a method like car.start() or car.brake(). name:Dodge is a key:value pair of the object car. Value is also
called a property. Thus Dodge:white is the property of the Dodge name.
<script>
 car={name:"Dodge", model:"Charger", color:"White", motor:"350Hemi"}
document.write(car.name +" "+ car.model +" "+ car.color +" "+ car.motor +"<br>");
</script>
OR to make it easier to read
<script>
 car={name:"Dodge", model:"Charger", color:"White", motor:"350Hemi"}
document.write(car.name +" "+ car.model +" "+ car.color +" "+ car.motor +"<br>");
</script>

Results below when ran in a script.
<script>
 car={name:"Dodge", model:"Charger", color:"White", motor:"350Hemi"}
document.write(car.name +", "+ car.model +", "+ car.color +", "+ car.motor +"<br>");
</script>

2nd way is declare a variable using the key word "new" Object(); followed by

objectname=value created key:value pair
Like this:
<script>
var amCar= new Object();
amCar.name="Ford";
amCar.model="Truck 150";
amCar.color="Blue Tone";
amCar.motor="3.5L Powerboost";
document.write(amCar.name +", "+ amCar.model +", "+ amCar.color +", "+ amCar.motor
+"<br>");
</script>
The above will yeild this below:
<script>
var amCar= new Object();
amCar.name="Ford";
amCar.model="Truck 150";
amCar.color="Blue Tone";
amCar.motor="3.5L Powerboost";
document.write(amCar.name +", "+ amCar.model +", "+ amCar.color +", "+ amCar.motor
+"<br>");
</script>

Third Way is to declare a function name (value1, value2, value3) and use
"this" a keyword to declare
the object names with the value then create a new simpler name for ease of writting it to the
screen. Like this.name=name
Then create a new personnel with id value of Chevy as below.
<script>
function cityCar(name, model, color, motor){
this.name=name;
this.model=model;
this.color=color;
this.motor=motor;
}
ccar=new cityCar("Chevy", "Corvette" , "Cherry Red", "6.2L LT2 V8");
document.write(ccar.name +", "+ ccar.model +", "+ ccar.color +", "+ ccar.motor +"<br>");

</script>
Now when we run the script and write to the HTML page you get the following.
<script>
function cityCar(name, model, color, motor){
this.name=name;
this.model=model;
this.color=color;
this.motor=motor;

```
}
ccar=new cityCar("Chevy", "Corvette" , "Cherry Red", "6.2L LT2 V8");
document.write(ccar.name +", "+ ccar.model +", "+ ccar.color +", "+ ccar.motor +"<br>");
</script>
```
Advantage to doing it this way you can create many instances of the same information by changing the input of one line like this:


```
<script>
function cityCar(name, model, color, motor){
this.name=name;
this.model=model;
this.color=color;
this.motor=motor;
}
ccar=new cityCar("Chevy", "Corvette" , "Cherry Red", "6.2L LT2 V8");
document.write(ccar.name +", "+ ccar.model +", "+ ccar.color +", "+ ccar.motor +"<br>");
ccar=new cityCar("Ford", "Truck F150" , "Blue Tone", "3.5L Powerboost");
document.write(ccar.name +", "+ ccar.model +", "+ ccar.color +", "+ ccar.motor +"<br>");
ccar=new cityCar("Dodge", "Charger" , "Pearl White", "350Hemi");
document.write(ccar.name +", "+ ccar.model +", "+ ccar.color +", "+ ccar.motor +"<br>");
</script>
```


The above script displayed:
*<script>
function cityCar(name, model, color, motor){
this.name=name;
this.model=model;
this.color=color;
this.motor=motor;
}
ccar=new cityCar("Chevy", "Corvette" , "Cherry Red", "6.2L LT2 V8");
document.write(ccar.name +", "+ ccar.model +", "+ ccar.color +", "+ ccar.motor +"<br>");

ccar=new cityCar("Ford", "Truck F150" , "Blue Tone", "3.5L Powerboost");
document.write(ccar.name +", "+ ccar.model +", "+ ccar.color +", "+ ccar.motor +"<br>");

ccar=new cityCar("Dodge", "Charger" , "Pearl White", "350Hemi");
document.write(ccar.name +", "+ ccar.model +", "+ ccar.color +", "+ ccar.motor +"<br>");

</script></i>
*

 Now there are two other ways to create Objects that will be covered in the advanced topics but basically
They are created automatically one is using a constructor and the other is by inheritance. The inheritance is the
Key to DOM the Domain Object Model that creates a Object of any HTML page and so anything displayed can

be accessed and displayed using these properties and methods of Objects. Also Objects can hold Objects, Arrays, and Functions as values
WHEW! Mind blowing like micro world inside of larger world inside a larger world hum is there space alien in the room?

Exercise: Write by hand the above italicized scripts into snippets.html and view in browser
Exercise: Copy and paste the scripts into snip.js

Now off to lesson 9 <a href="barebones9.html">Lesson 9 - DOM</a>
<p style="color:lightgray">
Reference: https://www.w3schools.com/js/js_htmldom.asp
Public Domain copywrite version 0 - Author retains rights to any additional versions or editions
Author: Brent Lichfield
</p>
</body>
</html>
****
barebones9.html
****
<!DOCTYPE html>
<html lang="en">
<head>
<title>
BareBones9
</title>
</head>
<body><p>
<h3>Mini-bootcamp BareBones Javascript</h3>
<h3>DOM</h3>
<h4>JavaScript HTML DOM</h4>
<p>Finding HTML Elements Using <b>document.forms</b>.</p>
When a web page is loaded, the browser creates a Document Object Model (DOM) of the page.
With the object model, JavaScript gets all the power it needs to create dynamic HTML or XML:
<ul>
<li>JavaScript can change all the HTML elements in the page</li>
<li>JavaScript can change all the HTML attributes in the page</li>
<li>JavaScript can change all the CSS styles in the page</li>
<li>JavaScript can remove existing HTML elements and attributes</li>
<li>JavaScript can add new HTML elements and attributes</li>
<li>JavaScript can react to all existing HTML events in the page</li>
<li>JavaScript can create new HTML events in the page</li>

</ul>

Because there are so many things that can be done obviously this is an advanced topic but a simple example will be given here.
We will show a form and create a paragraph with id of demo. We can use DOM to collect all the entries of the displayed form.
Because the form has several form inputs with different values we need a way to display those to the coder so he can create
some actions (methods) to present to the user. Remember the for loop previously discussed in Loops? That is how we get
the values out to display them via the following code. The rest of various uses will be discussed in an advanced discussion of
DOM but this helps you recognize the code. We will use the innerHTML method to display on the webpage.

<form id="frm1" action="action_page.html">
  First name: <input type="text" name="fname" value="Donald">
  Last name: <input type="text" name="lname" value="Duck">

  <input type="submit" value="Submit">
</form>

<p>Click on Submit then use the back arrow of the browser to return.
These are the values of each element in the form:
</p>

<p id="demo"></p>

<script>
const x = document.forms["frm1"];
let text = "";
for (let i = 0; i < x.length ;i++) {
  text += x.elements[i].value + "<br>";
}
document.getElementById("demo").innerHTML = text;
</script>
The script produced the text values using the <u>method</u> <b>document.forms</b> this scrapes the webpage form.
the const x = document.forms["frm1"]; created a object of the entire form tags and everything within them.
The for Loop then set i (incrementor) to zero then found the length of x then looped through the code block
The code block took var text and tested if the element had a value and if it did it concated that element with a
HTML return line then added 1 to the i and looped through again looking for another text value until done.

or x.length was met. At the end of code block the results of var text were displayed in the webpage.
When you clicked on the Submit button it carred out the actions within the form tags and the inputs
were sent another page to be pulled out and displayed.
<script>
const x = document.forms["frm1"];
let text = "";
for (let i = 0; i < x.length ;i++) {
  text += x.elements[i].value + "<br>";
}
document.getElementById("demo").innerHTML = text;
</script>

Exercise: Write by hand the above italicized scripts into snippets.html and view in browser
Exercise: Copy and paste the scripts into snip.js

Now off to lesson 10 <a href="barebones10.html">Lesson 10 Review and link to Advanced Topics</a>

Reference: https://www.w3schools.com/js/js_htmldom.asp
Public Domain copywrite version 0 - Author retains rights to any additional versions or editions
Author: Brent Lichfield

</body>
</html>

****
barebones10.html
****
<!DOCTYPE html>
<html lang="en">
<head>
<title>
BareBones10
</title>
</head>
<body>
<h3>Mini-bootcamp BareBones Javascript</h3>
<h3>Review</h3>
So for now let us do a review.

- <u>Introduction lesson taught:</u>
- You know what a **statement** is (commands using keywords that instruct the computer to do something).
- You know where to place the JavaScripts in the Body portion of the HTML page.
-       <**script>// Body JavaScript goes here</script>**
- You know you **view the code with MSNotepad** and see the **result using a brower like Chrome.**
- <u>1st lesson taught the following:</u>
- How to write your first line of JavaScript Code and displayed it in a browser html page
- You know how to create **comments** in the code (**// comment single line or /* much comment */**)
- **Snippets** are collections of code that perform something
- <u>2nd lesson introduced:</u>
- **Variables** and the syntax used to declare them like var a = equal to something followed by a semi-colon;
- **Syntax** is the <u>keyword</u> **var** used to declare them
- How to set a value to a variable is equal to **=** is the <u>keyword</u> **var a = "tom"; (as value).**
- <u>3rd lesson continued with:</u>
- **Operators and Math Syntax**
- **Operators** are used to <u>concate</u> or combine strings, or <u>substrings</u> is cut up strings
- **Math** is normal math computations
- **Incrementing** is a special adding of one to a number
- <u>4th lesson added:</u>
- **Strings and Arrays Syntax**
- **Strings** use length() to <u>concate</u> or combine strings, or <u>substrings</u> is cut up strings
- **Arrays** can hold a mix of value types and useful when doing something with the collection
- More about arrays later in advanced topics
- <u>5th lesson provided:</u>
- **Function Syntax**
- **Strings** **function() using curly brackets { //code; }**
- How to invoke or run a function
- More about functions later in advanced topics
- <u>6th lesson included:</u>
- **Flow control and Conditional Syntax**
- IF statements <script> var a = 12; if (a > 7){ /* execute the following lines of code */ alert(a); } </script>
- IF else statements
- var a = 12; if (a > 7){ /* execute the following lines of code */ alert(a); }else{ alert(b);}

```
<li> Conditionals for testing greater than or less than and others. More in advanced topics.</li>
<li><u>7th lesson instructed:</u></li>
<li> <b>Loop Syntax</b></li>
<li> loop  for statement </li>
<li>Using for statement to loop through same commands using a counter.</li>
<li><u>8th lesson introduced:</u></li>
<li> <b>Object Syntax</b></li>
<li>3 ways to create Objects </li>
<li>Objects can reside inside other Objects</li>
<li><u>9th lesson DOM simple example</u></li>
<li> <b>DOM Syntax example</b></li>
<li>Advanced topic with many more <b>methods</b></li>
<li>Example used for loop explained</li>
</ul>
<br> These are the major topics and syntax under Javascript. There are many more methods
and properties that can be <br>
discussed but these are major ones with a simple example explained. Now on to the Advanced
JavaScript Topics.<br>
</p>
<p>
Now Back to DOD  JS Handbook <a href="pageL0.html">Back to DOD-JS-Handbook Coding
without tools</a>
</p>
<p style="color:lightgray">

Public Domain copywrite version 0 - Author retains rights to any additional versions or
editions<br>
Author: Brent Lichfield
</p>
</body>
</html>


*******************************
pageL0.html
*******************************
<!DOCTYPE html>
<html lang="en">
<head>
<meta charset="utf-8">
<title>JS DOD-HB Page 0-1</title>
<style>//css goes here </style>
<SCRIPT LANGUAGE="Javascript">
// Javascript functions go here or in body
</SCRIPT>
```

```html
</head>
<body>
<center>
<h3>(JS) Javascript DOD HandBook</h3><br>
<h4>How to code without coding tools Page 0-1 </h4><br>
</center>
 <center><table><tr><td>     </td><td><button
class="HB"
   onclick="window.location.href = 'site_menu.html';">
     Site Menu
</button></td><td>     </td><td><button class="HB"
   onclick="window.location.href = 'lindex.html';">
     Begin Lessons
  </button></td><td>     </td><td><button class="HB"
   onclick="window.location.href = 'lindex.html';">
     Last Page
   </button></td><td>     </td><td><button class="HB"
   onclick="window.location.href = 'pageL1.html';">
     Next Page
   </button></td></tr></table></center>
<p><blockquote><blockquote><blockquote>
<h3>(JS) NOTEPAD & BROWSER</h3>
```

Welcome back from the barebones bootcamp on JavaScript. Nice little quickie about the basics of the JavaScript code. You might want to refer to it from time to time as we advance into the code. Hopefully this quickie will help you recognize the JavaScript code more readily and help you get more familiar with it. The bootcamp scratched the surface of Objects or DOM but we will get to that later. The advanced topics I will cover in the rest of the course are to help you to be able to spot the JavaScript code and fix it if needed. By now you know you "create" the source code using MSNotepad but "view the results" in a Brower like Chrome. `<br>`

`<p><blockquote>`Coders are also known as programmers. After all programmers are hired to fix broken code. With tools available today using templates you can build sites without knowing much code. Works good until something breaks. When it breaks you get both broken pieces to inspect. Like a a multilayered cake with various lanquages appearing on the screen. A programmer needs to recognize the Javascript, HTML, XML, CSS code, determine the cause, and get it back up and running properly.
 `<br><br>` This is meant to be just an introduction to the `<i>`basics `</i>`and not a full comprehensive study into Javascript. To awaken the coder inside of you. To help build confidence and understanding of how the language is used. Not everyone is meant to be a "coder", but for some it is almost like a gift from heaven. I hope this will help you determine if you have that gift. Get you on a path of daily trying out code and expanding your skills. Coding is useful to fix problems that arise, to have a basic understanding and recognition of the code when coders see it, then concentrate their efforts on the fix and not on the rebuild or rewrite from scratch.
`</blockquote></p>`
`<p><blockquote>`The interperter within (Igor) has set up some ground rules after all he

or she knows just a very <i>"little"</i> english. Certain <i> Keywords</i> or characters are reserved as commands and their meaning has to be agreed to. Or else the entire conversation would be chaotic. (Every computer language has it's own <i>terminalogy</i> for Javascript a command is called a "<b>statement</b>" and a <i>syntax </i>(specific order of words or appreviated words are arranged in the statement)). By using these commands we can instruct the computer to perform lots of manual mundane tasks in the blink of an eye.
 Javascript is an advanced language beyond the HTML (HyperText Markup Language) and CSS (Cascaded Style Sheets) languages also included in browers to display data and information. Knowing these two languages are critical to visualize your results. You can build stunning websites just knowing HTML and CSS. In addition the newer script coding tools run on a commercial website that build website and pages quickly still need skills in HTML and CSS when they fail. Not to mention the Javascript code that might be the failure reason. HTML does not interact with a user without another language. This advanced language is usually present on a webserver ("file server" that serves webpages). Javascripting is available on your PC or workstation as part of your browser.
 So how much do you need to know of HTML or CSS? I will try to keep it down to minimum, but to be proficient you will need to know these two languages as well; all three work together. HTML uses specific <> tags to instruct the web brower how to build the page for some one to see anything on the web screen. All html tags have a beginning<tag> and ending tag</tag>. The actual command is within these tags. There are about 30 commonly used commands with attributes that can be added to the command. I have built this quickie training in HTML if you wish refer to it. HTML Training <a href="htmlshell.html">HTML_short_training</a></p>
<p>
We will continue to use snip.js to add the code blocks within the script tags. The barebones start.html will be used to build your test pages to test your code like the snippet.html was used. But you might want to create your own test page using lesson1.html as a name for what you learned under lesson1 etc.

All website have a default starting page it is index.html you will want to build one for your site. The following is an example of simple navigation link you can add to your webpages to help move around your website. I advize you continue to hand input the commands in the script tags but it is optional to you from here on out.
      DOD-JavaScript-How to Code- Handbook <a href="lindex.html">   Menu Page <a href="site_menu.html"> Site Directory</a><p>   Begining Page <a href="index.html">Start page</a>   Previous Page <a href="lesson1.html"> Last page</a>   and Next Page <a href="lesson2.html">Next page</a></p>

The site_menu page will hold all the webpages used in the course. You can build your own site menu page with a different name to your lesson test pages.
</p>
OKAY go to Next Page.
</blockquote></p>
<SCRIPT LANGUAGE="Javascript">

```
// Javascript functions go here or in head
</SCRIPT>
<p> <center><table><tr><td>     </td><td><button
class="HB"
   onclick="window.location.href = 'site_menu.html';">
     Site Menu
</button></td><td>     </td><td><button class="HB"
   onclick="window.location.href = 'lindex.html';">
     Begin Lessons
  </button></td><td>     </td><td><button class="HB"
   onclick="window.location.href = 'lindex.html';">
     Last Page
  </button></td><td>     </td><td><button class="HB"
   onclick="window.location.href = 'pageL1.html';">
     Next Page
  </button></td></tr></table></center>
<p style="color:lightgray">
Public Domain copywrite &copy; version 0 - Author retains rights to any additional
versions or editions<br>
Author: Brent Lichfield
</p>
</blockquote></blockquote></blockquote>
</body>
</html>


********************************
pageL1.html
********************************
<!DOCTYPE HTML>
<HTML lang="en">
<head>
<meta charset="utf-8">
<title>JS DOD-HB Page 1</title>
<style>//CSS goes here </style>
<SCRIPT LANGUAGE="JavaScript">
// JavaScript functions go here or in body
</SCRIPT>
</head>
<body>
<center>
<h3>(JS) JavaScript DOD HandBook</h3><br>
<h4>JS DOD HandBook Page 1</h4><br>
</center>
 <center><table><tr><td>     </td><td><button
class="HB"
   onclick="window.location.href = 'site_menu.html';">
```

Site Menu
</button></td><td>   </td><td><button class="HB"
    onclick="window.location.href = 'lindex.html';">
    Begin Lessons
  </button></td><td>   </td><td><button class="HB"
    onclick="window.location.href = 'pageL0.html';">
    Last Page
  </button></td><td>   </td><td><button class="HB"
    onclick="window.location.href = 'pageL2.html';">
    Next Page
  </button></td></tr></table></center>
<p><blockquote><blockquote><blockquote><blockquote>

(JS) 1ST SCRIPT

<b><u>JavaScript LESSON 1 </u></b> your first command "<b>statement</b>" to your computer in JavaScript! Refresher from barebones bootcamp.
<i><script><b>document.write("Hello World!");</b></script></i>
So let's start with the basic building blocks of code. (Blocks of code are lines of JavaScript code that do something). The commands to Igor will now come from the translator or interpeter in JavaScript. Igor is ready watching the translator-interpeter. To give Igor a command you tell the interpeter by putting your commands inside the <i><script> command statement; </script></i> tags. JavaScript command statements <i><b>ALWAYS</b></i> terminated with a <b> ; </b>semicolon. This is what the interpeter is watching to know it has all the command statement. (<u>Note wise Student: </u>When a webpage does not provide what you expect <u>be sure your semicolons were not missing</u>). Your first command is to tell Igor to print to the webpage inside the body tags so anyone viewing the webpage will see the words Hello World. (Best practice is to put the <script> command statement </script> tags near the ending body tag.
 </body> like just above New Code Above line).

<i><script>
    document.write("Welcome World");
</script>
</i>

Copy and paste this to the lesson1.html then using the <i>browser</i> <u>view the results</u>.

IF Welcome World appeared in your page1.html browser. TATADA! You successfully wrote your first JavaScript program! You might be a JavaScript programmer yet! (Igor bowed and said yes master).

<script> document.write("Welcome World"); </script>

 Let us add another an alert box asking you to reply with a OKAY.
<i><script>alert("hi student are you enjoying this?");</script></i>
<script>alert("hi student are you enjoying this?");</script>

 There are three ways to display data on the webpage. 1st is to use document.write(variable); this has advantage of being quick and easy. Disadvantage is if something was displayed by HTML below this command it is erased. 2nd is to use a alert(); box this is popup box that displays an alert requiring user to click OKAY to proceed. Advantage is immediate interaction. Disadvantage it disappears after

acknowledgement. 3rd way is to use DOM (Domain Object Model) innerHTML statement (command).

 To use the DOM (Domain Object Model) statement **"document.getElementById("id").innerHTML = 5 + 6;"** method. In order for that to work you need to create a "id" in a HTML webpage like <p> *<p> id="demo" < /p >

   OR   <div></i>
 so JavaScript could use it.
id="demo" < /div >

</p>
 Good practice is to place this paragraph tag with a demo id (HTML tag) just below the opening body tag of the HTML page. In the template first line below body tags is area New Code so any paragraph tags would go just below that. You can then get JavaScript to print it using the id handle "demo" like below at the bottom of the HTML file just above the </body> tag.
*<p id="demo1"></p>
< script >
      document.getElementById("demo1").innerHTML = 5 + 6;
</script>
</i>
Result is 11 and this is the most common way used. (Note the <p> tags are not seen by users viewing the HTML file.) However **each line** or paragraph you wish to print to the webpage needs it's own HTML *"id"* element. The printing to the (screen) webpage often needs a *"trigger event"* or can be "invoked" commanded directly. Trigger event is a bit of code in a HTML tag directing when to execute the JavaScript. I will explain more later.

. You can use document.write() command to progress through the block of code to determine when a portion of the code failed to run. By using a JavaScript **Comment // **double forward slash will comment out one line of JavaScript code.
Plan on using the HTML<p> "id" method when ever possible to display to the webpage. But fast and dirty testing the *document.write();* command is used to test the code <p>The browsers have the JavaScript engine running at all times so if the engine sees a JavaScript in a **"trigger event"** and it recognizes a statement, then JavaScript will run that command without a formal scripting tags.</p><p>Like the following example:
 <p>JavaScript can change HTML attribute values.
Copy the following and add it to page1.HTML under the display here. Then refresh or open the webpage in your browser.

*<button onclick="document.getElementById('myImage').src='bulbon.jpg'">Turn on the light</button>

<img id="myImage" src="bulboff.jpg" style="width:100px">

<button onclick="document.getElementById('myImage').src='bulboff.jpg'">Turn off the light</button>

</i>

This is done with button HTML tags and just the single JavaScript embedded statement onclick="document.getElementById('myImage').src=bulbon.jpg or src=bulboff.jpg
<button onclick="document.getElementById('myImage').src='bulbon.jpg'">Turn on the light</button> <img id="myImage" src="bulboff.jpg" style="width:100px"> <button

onclick="document.getElementById('myImage').src='bulboff.jpg'">Turn off the light</button>

</p>
 but as you can see there are no formal scripting tags being used.< script >

< /script >

Like in this lesson a event of "onclick" in the webpage tag modifies the image displayed by a JavaScript DOM code.
The ability to <i>trigger on a event</i> enables interaction with the user viewing or inputting something on the page. Often these trigger events call <i>functions</i> with a list of command statements within them.
At the top of the page the first example of a JavaScript "Welcome World" is displayed inside the HTML <i>script</i> tags.

<p>JavaScript code can be embedded inside head section or body section of a HTML page. But best practice is to put it at the bottom of the body. Exceptions are usually when a "OFF The Shelf" commercial code has placed their JavaScript in the head section.</p>

<p>
Computer program is a list of "instructions" to be "executed" by a computer in 8 binary bits of zeros and ones, 01010100 computer speak. The onboard JavaScript compiler converts to computer speak. This list is sequential 1st line, next line, and so forth by default, each line is terminated by ";". But there are some flow control methods and keywords we will discuss later. In JavaScript these executable commands are called statements. Statements can have within them Values, Operators, Expressions, Keywords, and Comments. JavaScript statements can be grouped together in code blocks. Common code blocks are functions. Will discuss functions later.
<p>
Go To Next Page
</blockquote><blockquote><blockquote><blockquote><blockquote></p>
 <center><table><tr><td>   </td><td><button class="HB"
   onclick="window.location.href = 'site_menu.html';">
     Site Menu
</button></td><td>   </td><td><button class="HB"
   onclick="window.location.href = 'lindex.html';">
     Begin Lessons
  </button></td><td>   </td><td><button class="HB"
   onclick="window.location.href = 'pageL0.html';">
     Last Page
   </button></td><td>   </td><td><button class="HB"
   onclick="window.location.href = 'pageL2.html';">
     Next Page
   </button></td></tr></table></center>

<p style="color:lightgray">
Public Domain copywrite © version 0 - Author retains rights to any additional versions or editions
Author: Brent Lichfield

```
</p>
</body>
</html>
```

```
*******************************
pageL2.html
*******************************
<html >
<head>
<title>JS-HB Page2</title>
<style>//CSS goes here</style>
<script>//JavaScript goes here</script>
</head>
<body>
<h3>)(JS) JavaScript DOD HandBook</h3>
<h4>How to code without coding tools Page 2 </h4>
 <center><table><tr><td>     </td><td><button
class="HB"
   onclick="window.location.href = 'site_menu.html';">
     Site Menu
</button></td><td>     </td><td><button class="HB"
   onclick="window.location.href = 'lindex.html';">
     Begin Lessons
   </button></td><td>     </td><td><button class="HB"
   onclick="window.location.href = 'pageL1.html';">
     Last Page
   </button></td><td>     </td><td><button class="HB"
   onclick="window.location.href = 'pageL3.html';">
     Next Page
   </button></td></tr></table></center>
```

```
<p><blockquote><blockquote><blockquote><blockquote>
<h3>)(JS) USING .JS FILE</h3>
```
Okay let us press on with <u>Lesson 2</u> How to Seperate JavaScript from
HTML
JavaScript command statements can be held in a seperate file than the HTML tags.
<script src=myjsFile.js></script> here is an example where the script will look
for a file named myjsFile.js within the same folder as the html file. Remember you
created a snip.js holding all the scripts from the barebones bootcamp. Create your
lesson2.html file. Create a new .js file with a name of jshb.js

We will fill it with a block of code; copy and paste below to jshb.js then save the
additions.

document.write("<br>");
document.write("
Creating a variable called robot using let command instead of

var
");
document.write("Text string in memory position robot
");
let robot = "R2CPO";
document.write(robot);
document.write("<br>");
var name1 = "<img src=F35.jpg width=200 height=200 alt=F35_Image>";
document.write("
A picture in memory position name1?
");
document.write(name1);
document.write("<br>");
document.write("Technically the picture is not stored in name1. What is stored is the
HTML command to display the file F35.jpg.
");
Insert the above code adding to JSHandBook.js (remember to save the changes) to the
bottom and refresh the page2.HTML.

 So copy the following and add it to your JSHandBook.js and save.
document.write("<br>");
document.write("
 declaring a constant variable interestRate with 30 percent
rate
");
const interestRate = 0.3;
document.write(interestRate);
document.write("<br>");
document.write("
trying to set this rate to different interest rate by this name will
cause JavaScript engine to crash
");
document.write("
visually you would see nothing in the new code lines as
JavaScript would fail not even the picture would show up.
");
document.write("<br>");

<p>Add a new script in Lesson2.html save and view with a browser

<script src="jshb.js">
</script>

<u>The WHOLE purpose of the exercise above is to help you as a coder
understand where your command statements are located. Generally
they are located within script tags in the HTML but they might be in a seperate .js
file.</u> And you can use this technique to seperate the two types of code.

Exercise: Use comments to eliminate lines of code // is a comment or /* lots of lines
of code */ view results in your lesson2.html
This technique is used to troubleshoot when you have added blocks of code and
something is failing to print or give expected results.
It will help you narrow the code down to a line or two to concentrate your fixing skills.

</p>
</blockquote></blockquote></blockquote></blockquote>
Go to Next Page</p>

<script>//JavaScript goes here</script>

```html
 <center><table><tr><td>     </td><td><button
class="HB"
   onclick="window.location.href = 'site_menu.html';">
     Site Menu
</button></td><td>     </td><td><button class="HB"
   onclick="window.location.href = 'lindex.html';">
     Begin Lessons
  </button></td><td>     </td><td><button class="HB"
   onclick="window.location.href = 'pageL1.html';">
     Last Page
  </button></td><td>     </td><td><button class="HB"
   onclick="window.location.href = 'pageL3.html';">
     Next Page
  </button></td></tr></table></center>
<p style="color:lightgray">
Public Domain copywrite &copy; version 0 - Author retains rights to any additional
versions or editions<br>
Author: Brent Lichfield
</p></body>
</html>
```

****

pageL3.html

****

```html
<!DOCTYPE HTML>
<HTML lang="en">
<head>
<meta charset="utf-8">
<title>JS-HB Page3</title>
<style>//CSS goes here</style>
</head>
<body>
<h3>(JS) Javascript DOD HandBook</h3>
<h4>How to code without coding tools Page 3</h4>
 <center><table><tr><td>     </td><td><button
class="HB"
   onclick="window.location.href = 'site_menu.html';">
     Site Menu
</button></td><td>     </td><td><button class="HB"
   onclick="window.location.href = 'lindex.html';">
     Begin Lessons
  </button></td><td>     </td><td><button class="HB"
   onclick="window.location.href = 'pageL2.html';">
     Last Page
  </button></td><td>     </td><td><button class="HB"
   onclick="window.location.href = 'pageL4.html';">
```

Next Page
```
</button></td></tr></table></center>
<blockquote><blockquote><blockquote>
<p id="demo1"></p>
<p id="demo2"></p>
```
(JS) VARIABLES

HTML webpages shows us how the page would appear to the user. It is just a picture or window. To be truely useful we need to be able
interact with the user, obtain input, and relay that to a file webserver, who will respond back with another webpage. Javascript is how
interaction is done. In HTML you can create forms, buttons, check marks, that are used to get input from the user. But to pass this information
across the vast space of the internet you need a program language to bundle the information and send it in a transmission to the file webserver.
The webserver will extract the input and get information from a backend server database or just store it in a front end server to interact with
the user PC and display a new or updated webpage. There are many web programming languages but Javascript uses the resources of the
user's PC to check for data accuracy and format the data properly. This relieves the webserver of those duties, memory, and resources.
Eliminating lots of work and communications overhead without it. This is why it is so popular and widely used. Most of the
coding is done within functions, whole lesson about that ahead.

<p><u>What is a Variable?</u>
All programming languages use this term "variable", in Javascript it is a temporary memory location within the user's PC (RAM-Read,Access-Memory).
 How we create this location is we give it a name. It will hold whatever we input into it and we can call this location and it's contents for use by
 referencing the name. Remember you asked (Igor your computer) "get me data", Igor responded with Huh or 10111111 or ?.
That is because Igor saw the request but did not know what to do with it when he got it in the nano seconds it took him or her.
That is approximately 1 millionth of one millionth of one second.
Using a variable declaration tells Igor to store the data.

 Refresher from barebones bootcamp.
<script>
var newline = "<br>";
var mess1 = "myVariable is now ";
var mess2 = "Changed myVariable to ";
var myVar = 5;
document.write(mess1);
document.write(newline);
document.write(myVar);
// result = 5
<script>
Result


```
<script>
var newline = "<br>";
var mess1 = "myVariable is now ";
var mess2 = "Changed myVariable to ";
var myVar = 5;
document.write(mess1);
document.write(newline);
document.write(myVar);
// result = 5
</script><br>
```
Variables <b> can NOT</b> begin with numbers or contain spaces, letters and but certain special characters can be used.
Variables are <b>case sensitive</b> like yourname and yourName are not the same.
Variables are created using var
a keyword to declare a variable or create a variable. You can assign a value to them like var myName = "Mike"
and does not matter if var myNumber = 5; as variables use primative letters and numbers organically.
I could change myName to a number by var myName = 50; No error because this is acceptable.
Variables names should use "camel notation" var myName like a camel hump
So what is under the hood within the script tags?

<i><script>// Body script tag Javascript Code goes here
var myName = "Mike";
myNumber = 5;
document.write(myName + "<br>" + myNumber + "<br>");
myName = 50;
myNumber = "Sarah";
document.write(myName + "<br>" + myNumber + "<br>");
</script></i>


```
<script>// Body script tag Javascript Code goes here
var myName = "Mike";
myNumber = 5;
document.write(myName + "<br>" + myNumber + "<br>");
myName = 50;
myNumber = "Sarah";
document.write(myName + "<br>" + myNumber + "<br>");
</script><br>
```

 In Javascript there are rules. Rules help everyone play in sand box together; just like in any other society we must operate within the rules.

<u>Rule One: </u> Variables cannot use a reserved word. Like "IF" or "Let" these reserved names are part of Javascript commands. Rules if used
 improperly the interpeter will give you a error. Usually with a line number of where it saw the error.

<a href="keywords.HTML"> Key Words (Reserved) LINK </a> You can NOT use a key word as a variable.
<u>Rule Two:</u> Variable names should be meaningful and descriptive. Short names like a1 does not meet this rule.
<u>Rule Three: </u>Variable names cannot begin with a number.
<u>Rule Four:</u> Variable names cannot contain a space   or a hyphen "-".When using meaningful names that are word combinations create single word.
<u>Rule Five:</u> Variable names should use camel notation. Camel notation is when combining words like first name; the combination would start with
lower case letter and second word would use a capilatization. Like "firstName". (Like a camel hump).
<u>Rule Six:</u> Variable names are case sensitive so "FirstName" and "firstName" are not the same, using camel notation will avoid this.
<u>Rule Seven: </u>You can declare more than one variable on one line. This is done by seperating each variable by a comma.
Such as let firstName = 'Ken', lastName = 'Bartlet'; is declaring two variables firstName and lastName <br> and you can add more <i>statements</i> on the same line seperated by comma.
However best practice is to use a single line for each declaration of a variable to ease in reading the program or programmer understanding.
 There is another word we can use to declare a variable. It is const this means that once declared the variable is constant and is unchangeable.
 Variables can also be bound to a container area like in functions. This called being "block scoped"
Meaning they cannot be used in a global or universal block if declared inside a function.General rule those declared outside of function
are global variables unless passed as result of the function or a window statement. <a href="var_global.html"> Global variables </a>
some examples.

Go to Next Page

 <table><tr><td>   </td><td><button class="HB"
   onclick="window.location.href = 'site_menu.html';">
     Site Menu
</button></td><td>   </td><td><button class="HB"
   onclick="window.location.href = 'lindex.html';">
     Begin Lessons
  </button></td><td>   </td><td><button class="HB"
   onclick="window.location.href = 'pageL2.html';">
     Last Page
  </button></td><td>   </td><td><button class="HB"
   onclick="window.location.href = 'pageL4.html';">
     Next Page
  </button></td></tr></table>

</blockquote></blockquote></blockquote><p>

<p style="color:lightgray">
Public Domain copywrite © version 0 - Author retains rights to any additional
versions or editions
Author: Brent Lichfield
</p>
</body>
</html>

```
*******************************
pageL4.html
*******************************
<!DOCTYPE HTML>
<HTML lang="en">
<head>
<meta charset="utf-8">
<title>Page 4</title>
<style>//CSS goes here</style>
<SCRIPT LANGUAGE="Javascript">
// Javascript functions go here or in body
</SCRIPT>
</head>
<body>
<h3>(JS) Javascript DOD HandBook</h3>
<h4>How to code without coding tools Page 4</h4><br>
 <center><table><tr><td>     </td><td><button
class="HB"
   onclick="window.location.href = 'site_menu.html';">
     Site Menu
</button></td><td>     </td><td><button class="HB"
   onclick="window.location.href = 'lindex.html';">
     Begin Lessons
  </button></td><td>     </td><td><button class="HB"
   onclick="window.location.href = 'pageL3.html';">
     Last Page
  </button></td><td>     </td><td><button class="HB"
   onclick="window.location.href = 'pageL5.html';">
     Next Page
  </button></td></tr></table></center>
<h3>(JS) MATH vs CONDITIONALS</h3>
<p><b>Lesson 3 Functions</b> <br>
</lockquote></lockquote><blockquote>
<br><u>Variables use <b>Operators</b> and <i>Conditionals</i></u> to create
decisions for the computer program. Below are a few examples.<br>
Operand are the number(s) used in math, <b> operators </b>are +, -, *, /, **,%   used in
```

computer math. We normally declare a variable and assign
a value like var a=1; and var b=2; we then use a operator to get a sum like var
sumr = a + b; then use document.write = sumr; or
 getElementbyId(demo); to
display it on the website. Or var suma = a * b; if we were multiplying or doing other
math activity.
<a href="math.HTML"> Javascript Math</a>
The + operator can also be used to concatenate meaning to join. Used to create single
strings into one large string.
The common use you have seen in document.write(" Shoot me" + " to the moon"); to
write to the webpage. The + is a concatenation.
Concatenation can combine strings and numbers like var mission=14; document.write("
Appollo" + mission +" to the moon");
Would print out "Appollo14 to the moon".
Conditional Operators are also used in conditional statements to determine if something
is true or false, exactly alike or not alike.
And what to do after determining the condition. These are often inside a function
showing what statements to execute if a condition is
true or if condition is false.
Conditional statements are like If (a greater than b) { document.write = " a is greater
than b";} (Example of a IF statement).
In JavaScript they are written like this: If(condition){ then command statements in
turn;}
If condition is not true then go to next command statement in the list of statements in
turn. Statement1,
 IF statement(a greater than b){ statement2 = true, statement2 = false go to next
statement outside the IF }
Statement 3, Statement 4, Statement 5.
In actual coding writing it would be easier to understand if you write it like this.
Statement1,
 IF statement(a greater than b){ statement 2 = true, document.write ("true"),statement
2= false go to next statement outside the IF }
Statement 3,
Statement 4,
Statement 5.

Conditionals create decision choices and the statements used are associated with the
choice true or false or other choices.
Conditionals are listed below.
 If (some condition){statements;} syntax.
<ul>
<li>Each condition yields either true or false NOT the result like an assignment.</li>
<li>Greater/less than: a > b, a < b.</li>
<li>Greater/less than or equals: a >= b, a <= b.</li>
<li>Equals: a == b, please note the double equality sign == means the equality test,
while a single one a = b means an assignment.</li>
<li>Exact Equals: a === b, tests first if the letters converted to numbers are equal then
tests each character as exact same in Unicode not dictionary!</li>

<li>Not equals: In math the notation is ≠, but in JavaScript it's written as a != b.</li>
</ul>
We can have several conditional statements chained together with keywords that permit more than one outcome or a series of outcomes
before a condition is met.
A switch break condition is where there a series of conditional statements that use the break key word
 to stop the flow when a condition is met.Today is Wednesday

Wednesday is third day of the work week
Wednesday is the day the computer recognizes as the Day number within object Date

Looking forward to the Weekend

So looking at the script.

```
<script> let day; switch (new Date().getDay()) { case 0: day = "Sunday";
document.getElementById("demo1").innerHTML = "Sunday is first day of the week <br>
";
break; case 1: day = "Monday"; document.getElementById("demo2").innerHTML =
"Monday is first day of the work week <br> ";
break; case 2: day = "Tuesday"; document.getElementById("demo3").innerHTML =
"Tuesday is second day of the work week <br> ";
break; case 3: day = "Wednesday"; document.getElementById("demo4").innerHTML =
"Wednesday is third day of the work week <br> ";
break; case 4: day = "Thursday"; document.getElementById("demo5").innerHTML =
"Thursday is fourth day of the work week <br> ";
break; case 5: day = "Friday"; document.getElementById("demo6").innerHTML =
"Friday is 5th day of the work week <br> ";
break; case 6: document.getElementById("demo7").innerHTML = "Saturday is first day
of the weekend <br> ";
day = "Saturday"; }
document.getElementById("demo").innerHTML = "Today is " + day;
document.getElementById("demo8").innerHTML = "" + day + " is the day the computer
recognizes as the Day number within object Date";
let text; switch (new Date().getDay()) {
default: text = "Looking forward to the Weekend"; break;
case 6: text = "Today is Saturday"; break;
case 0: text = "Today is Sunday";
}
document.getElementById("demo9").innerHTML = text;
</script>
```

The getDay() method returns the weekday as a number between 0 and 6.
(Sunday=0, Monday=1, Tuesday=2 ..)
This example uses the weekday number to calculate the weekday name:
When JavaScript reaches a break keyword, it breaks out of the switch block.
This will stop the execution inside the switch block.

It is not necessary to break the last case in a switch block. The block breaks (ends) there anyway.

A if else if condition uses conditionals to get the correct result.
 if (condition1){ command statements to perform if true;}
else if(condition2){ command statements to perform if true;}
else if(condition3){ command statements to perform if true;}
else if(condition4){ command statements to perform if true;}
else if(condition n){ command statements to perform if true;}
else {command statements to perform by default if no condition is matched;}

Look at this code.
<script>
  var book = "maths";
document.write("
var = maths, testing for maths, economics, and history books
");
  if(book == "history") {
   document.write("<b>History Book</b>");
  } else if(book == "maths") {
   document.write("<b>Maths Book</b>");
  } else if(book == "economics") {
   document.write("<b>Economics Book</b>");
  } else {
   document.write("<b>Unknown Book</b>");// default
  }
</script>
 <script>
<!--
  var book = "maths";
document.write("
var = maths, testing for maths, economics, and history books</br>");
  if(book == "history") {
   document.write("<b>History Book</b>");
  } else if(book == "maths") {
   document.write("<b>Maths Book</b>");
  } else if(book == "economics") {
   document.write("<b>Economics Book</b>");
  } else {
   document.write("<b>Unknown Book</b>");
  }
//-->
 </script>
 <p>Set the variable to different value and then try...</p>

There are more complex conditional statements used in Arrays and Objects like
<b>loops for, for of, for in, for each, while loops.</b>
The most commonly used loop is for loops as in the barebones bootcamp. More on that

later as Decision loop discussion. </a>

NEXT PAGE
</p>
<p>

</p>
</blockquote></blockquote></blockquote>
<SCRIPT LANGUAGE="Javascript">
// Javascript functions go here or in head
</SCRIPT>
 <center><table><tr><td>   </td><td><button
class="HB"
   onclick="window.location.href = 'site_menu.html';">
      Site Menu
</button></td><td>   </td><td><button class="HB"
   onclick="window.location.href = 'lindex.html';">
      Begin Lessons
  </button></td><td>   </td><td><button class="HB"
   onclick="window.location.href = 'pageL3.html';">
      Last Page
   </button></td><td>   </td><td><button class="HB"
   onclick="window.location.href = 'pageL5.html';">
      Next Page
   </button></td></tr></table></center>

<p style="color:lightgray">
Public Domain copywrite © version 0 - Author retains rights to any additional
versions or editions
Author: Brent Lichfield
</p>
</body>
</html>

****
pageL5.html
****
<!DOCTYPE html>
<html lang="en">
<head>
<meta charset="utf-8">
<title>Page 5</title>
<style>//CSS goes here</style>
<SCRIPT LANGUAGE="JavaScript">
// javascript functions go here or in body

```
</SCRIPT>
</head>
<body>
<h3>(JS) Javascript DOD HandBook</h3>
<h4>How to code without coding tools Page 5</h4>
 <center><table><tr><td>     </td><td><button
class="HB"
   onclick="window.location.href = 'site_menu.html';">
      Site Menu
</button></td><td>     </td><td><button class="HB"
   onclick="window.location.href = 'lindex.html';">
      Begin Lessons
  </button></td><td>     </td><td><button class="HB"
   onclick="window.location.href = 'pageL4.html';">
      Last Page
  </button></td><td>     </td><td><button class="HB"
   onclick="window.location.href = 'pageL6.html';">
      Next Page
  </button></td></tr></table></center>
<h3>(JS) Strings</h3>
<blockquote><blockquote><blockquote>
<p>
<u>Strings</u> are actually characters or words and stored as <u>Objects</u>.
Meaning they have a lot of hidden properties.<br> Objects can have many properties
and values (attributes) tied to each property. The hidden values take advanced
coding.<br>
Strings internal properties includes <b>length() and substring() </b>. These are
accessed by variable name <br>
"." or dot length or "." dot substring like this var length = alpha.length for variable
alpha="abcdefg";<br>
length will return the number of characters in the variable value in this case it will be
7.<br>
Substring(x,y) takes two inputs, 1st character to start the count, and 2nd character to
end the count<br>
like var newalpha = alpha.substring(2,6); would give you cdef as a result. (Begin with
0).<br>
This is known as a "<b>Method</b>" meaning it takes and calculates a result based on
a property. <br>
<br> Code in the script tags:<br>
<i>&lt;script&gt;  <br>
var newline = "&lt;br&gt;"; <br>
var alength = "Length of the variable value";<br>
var alpha = "ABCDEFG";<br>
var length = alpha.length;<br>
document.write(alength); <br>
document.write(newline);<br>
```

```
document.write(length);<br>
document.write(newline);<br>
var newalpha = alpha.substring(2,6);<br>
document.write(alpha); <br>
document.write(newline);<br>
document.write(newalpha);<br>
document.write(newline);<br>
&lt;/script&gt;</i><br>
Yields the following:<br>
</p>
<script>
var newline = "<br>";
var alength = "Length of the variable value";
var alpha = "ABCDEFG";
var length = alpha.length;
document.write(alength);
document.write(newline);
document.write(length);
document.write(newline);
var newalpha = alpha.substring(2,6);
document.write(alpha);
document.write(newline);
document.write(newalpha);
document.write(newline);
</script>
```

Concatenate means to link together or add to the end of the string.var randString = "A long " + "string that " + "goes on and on and on" 3 strings together. Get the Index for \"goes\" : we use the back slash \ to quote a " quotation inside the document write command. randString.indexOf("goes") searches the string for the first "goes".

```
    <script>// Body Javascript Code goes here
document.write("Concatenate the string " + "<br>");
var randString = "A Long " + "string that " + "goes on and on and on";
document.write("Concatenating randString = " , randString , "<br>");
document.write(" Get the string length with variable.length  " + "<br>");
document.write("String Length = " , randString.length , "<br>");
document.write(" Get the Index for \"goes\" :  " + "<br>");
document.write("Index for \"goes\" = " , randString.indexOf("goes") , "<br>");
document.write("randString sliced at 19 to 23  = " , randString.slice(19, 23) , "<br>");
document.write("randString sliced  at 19 to end  = " , randString.slice(19) , "<br>");
document.write("randString substring at 19 and for next 8 characters  = " ,
randString.substr(19,8) , "<br>");
document.write("randString replace that for is forever and  = " ,
randString.replace("that","is forever and") , "<br>");
document.write("At Index 2  = " , randString.charAt(2) , "<br>");
document.write("At Index 1  = " , randString.charAt(1) , "<br>");
document.write("At Index 0   since counting is from 0 = " , randString.charAt(0) , "<br>");
```

```
</script>
<script>
var randStr = "A Long " + "string that " + "goes on and on and on";
var randStrArray = randStr.split(" ");
document.write("randStr  converted to an array split at space  randStrArray = " ,
randStrArray , "<br>");
document.write("randStr you can strip whitespace front and end with randStr trim = " ,
randStr.trim() , "<br>");
document.write(" Upper Case = " , randStr.toUpperCase() , "<br>");
document.write(" Lower Case = " , randStr.toLowerCase() , "<br>");
</script>
<script>
document.write("Styling your strings " + "<br>");
var strToStyle = "Random String";
document.write("Big : " , strToStyle.big() , "<br>");
document.write("Bold : " , strToStyle.bold() , "<br>");
document.write("Font Color : " , strToStyle.fontcolor("blue") , "<br>");
document.write("Font Size : " , strToStyle.fontsize("14em") , "<br>");
document.write("Italics : " , strToStyle.italics() , "<br>");
document.write("Google link : " , strToStyle.link("http://google.com") , "<br>");
document.write("Small : " , strToStyle.small() , "<br>");
document.write("Strike : " , strToStyle.strike() , "<br>");
document.write("Sub : " , strToStyle.sub() , "<br>");
document.write("Sup : " , strToStyle.sup() , "<br>");
</script>
<h1>JavaScript String Methods</h1>
<p>Convert string to upper case:</p>

<button onclick="myFunctiona()">Try All Upper Case</button>

<p id="demo">Hello World!</p>

<script>
function myFunctiona() {
  let text = document.getElementById("demo").innerHTML;
  document.getElementById("demo").innerHTML =
  text.toUpperCase();
}
</script>
<p>Convert string to lower case:</p>

<button onclick="myFunctionb()">Try lowercase</button>

<p id="demo1">GoodBye World!</p>

<script>
```

```
function myFunctionb() {
  let text = document.getElementById("demo1").innerHTML;
  document.getElementById("demo1").innerHTML =
  text.toLowerCase();
}
</script>
<button onclick="myFunctionc()">Back to Upper Case</button>

<p id="demo2">hello world, goodbye world!</p>

<script>
function myFunctionc() {
  let text = document.getElementById("demo2").innerHTML;
  document.getElementById("demo2").innerHTML =
  text.toUpperCase();
}
</script>
<p>The concat() method joins two or more strings:</p>

<p id="demo4"></p>
<p id="demo5"></p>
<p id="demo6"></p>
<script>
let text1 = "Hello";
let text2 = "World!";
let text3 = text1.concat(" ",text2);
document.getElementById("demo4").innerHTML = text3;
text4 = "Hello" + " " + "Tom!";
document.getElementById("demo5").innerHTML = text4 + "You have seen how to join
two strings using plus signs";
text5 = "Hello".concat(" ", "Tommy!");
document.getElementById("demo6").innerHTML = text5+ "You can do it with concat
command as well";
</script>
<p id=demo5a> The trim() method is used to eliminate extra white space that are often
invisiable hard to convert to numbers without taking out spaces first.</p>

<p id="demo6"></p>

<script>
let text11 = "    Hello World!     ";
let text12 = text11.trim();

document.getElementById("demo6").innerHTML =
"Length text11 = " + text11.length + "<br>Length text12 = " + text12.length + "
<br>When you just want the value inside a string use trim";
```

```
</script>
```

<p id=demo7> There are Newer trim() methods since 2019 but may not be loaded in the browser versions of Standard Desktop Computer used by DOD.</p>
<p>Display the first array element, after a string split:
using const myArray = text.split(","); to create a new array using the comma as split value.
This is called up by myArray[0] reference to the first value in the array at point 0. + " a is first character in text = a,b,c,d,e,f"</p>

<p id="demo"></p>
<p id="demo1"></p>
<p id="demo2"></p>
<p id="demo3"></p>
<p id="demo4"></p>
<p id="demo5"></p>
<p id="demo6"></p>
<p id="demo7"></p>
<p id="demo8"></p>
<p id="demo9"></p>
<p id="demo10"></p>
<p id="demo11"></p>
<p id="demo12"></p>

```
<script>
let text = "a,b,c,d,e,f";
const myArray = text.split(",");
document.getElementById("demo").innerHTML = myArray[0];
</script>
<script>
let texta = "a|b|c|d|e|f";
const myArraya = texta.split("|");
document.getElementById("demo2").innerHTML = myArraya[1];
document.getElementById("demo1").innerHTML = "The pipe | used as a split value
texta = a|b|c|d|e|f and 2nd character <br>";
</script>
<script>
let textb = "a b c d e f";
const myArrayb = textb.split(" ");
document.getElementById("demo4").innerHTML = myArrayb[2];
document.getElementById("demo3").innerHTML = "The space used as a split value
texta = a b c d e f and 3rd character [2] <br>";
</script>
<script>
let textc = "alpha,beta,charley,delta,echo,foxtrot";
document.getElementById("demo5").innerHTML =" text is equal to " + textc;
const myArrayc = textc.split(",");
```

```
document.getElementById("demo7").innerHTML = myArrayc[0];
document.getElementById("demo6").innerHTML = "The comma used as a split value
textc = alpha,beta,charley,delta,echo,foxtrot; and 4th character [0] <br>a string can be
one character or to infinity and beyond! an array itself can have infinity individual
references to characters";
</script>
<script>
let textd = "a &b &c &d &e &f";
const myArrayd = textd.split("&");
document.getElementById("demo9").innerHTML = myArrayd[3];
document.getElementById("demo8").innerHTML = "The & used as a split value texta =
a &b &c &d &e &f and 4th character [3] <br>";
</script>
<script>
let texte = "a,b,c,d,e,f";
const myArraye = texte.split("");
document.getElementById("demo10").innerHTML = myArraye[5] + " text equal to
a,b,c,d,e,f empty paramater in the split gives comma";
let textf = "a,b,c,d,e,f";
const myArrayf = textf.split();
document.getElementById("demo11").innerHTML = myArrayf[5] + " no paramater in the
split gives undefined";
<h2>toString()</h2>
<p>The toString() method returns an array as a comma separated string:</p>

<p id="demo"></p>
<p> script command statements: <br>
const fruits = ["Banana", "Orange", "Apple", "Mango"];<br>
document.getElementById("demo").innerHTML = fruits.toString();<br></p>
<script>
const fruits = ["Banana", "Orange", "Apple", "Mango"];
document.getElementById("demo").innerHTML = fruits.toString();
</script>
<p>The join() method joins array elements into a string.</p>
<p>It this example we have used " * " as a separator between the elements:</p>

<p id="demo1"></p>
<p id="demo2"></p>
<script>
const fruit = ["Banana", "Orange", "Apple", "Mango"];
document.getElementById("demo1").innerHTML = fruit.join(" * ");
document.getElementById("demo2").innerHTML = fruit;
</script>
<p> script command statements: <br>
const fruit = ["Banana", "Orange", "Apple", "Mango"];<br>
document.getElementById("demo1").innerHTML = fruit.join(" * ");<br>
```

document.getElementById("demo2").innerHTML = fruit;</p>

<p>The pop() method removes the last element from an array.</p>
<p> script command statements:
const fruite = ["Banana", "Orange", "Apple", "Mango"];
document.getElementById("demo3").innerHTML = fruite;
fruite.pop();
document.getElementById("demo4").innerHTML = fruite;</p>
<p id="demo3"></p>
<p id="demo4"></p>
<script>
const fruite = ["Banana", "Orange", "Apple", "Mango"];
document.getElementById("demo3").innerHTML = fruite;
fruite.pop();
document.getElementById("demo4").innerHTML = fruite;
</script>
<p>The pop() method in the print statement prints the item removed as the last element from an array. Then displays array.</p>
<p> script command statements:
const fruita = ["Banana", "Orange", "Apple", "Kiwi"];
document.getElementById("demo5").innerHTML = fruita.pop();
fruite.pop();
document.getElementById("demo4").innerHTML = fruita;</p>
<p id="demo5"></p>
<p id="demo6"></p>
<script>
const fruita = ["Banana", "Orange", "Apple", "Kiwi"];
document.getElementById("demo5").innerHTML = fruita.pop();
document.getElementById("demo6").innerHTML = fruita;
</script>
</blockquote></blockquote></blockquote>
 <center><table><tr><td>   </td><td><button class="HB"
   onclick="window.location.href = 'site_menu.html';">
     Site Menu
</button></td><td>   </td><td><button class="HB"
   onclick="window.location.href = 'lindex.html';">
     Begin Lessons
  </button></td><td>   </td><td><button class="HB"
   onclick="window.location.href = 'pageL4.html';">
     Last Page
  </button></td><td>   </td><td><button class="HB"
   onclick="window.location.href = 'pageL6.html';">
     Next Page
  </button></td></tr></table></center>

<p style="color:lightgray">
Public Domain copywrite © version 0 - Author retains rights to any additional versions or editions
Author: Brent Lichfield
</p>
</body>
</html>

****

pageL6.html
****
<!DOCTYPE html>
<html lang="en">
<head>
<meta charset="utf-8">
<title>Page 6</title>
<style>//CSS goes here</style>
<SCRIPT LANGUAGE="JavaScript">
// javascript functions go here or in body
</SCRIPT>
</head>
<body>
<h3>(JS) Javascript DOD HandBook</h3>
<h4>How to code without coding tools Page 6</h4>
 <center><table><tr><td>   </td><td><button class="HB"
   onclick="window.location.href = 'site_menu.html';">
     Site Menu
</button></td><td>   </td><td><button class="HB"
   onclick="window.location.href = 'lindex.html';">
     Begin Lessons
  </button></td><td>   </td><td><button class="HB"
   onclick="window.location.href = 'pageL5.html';">
     Last Page
    </button></td><td>   </td><td><button class="HB"
   onclick="window.location.href = 'pageL7.html';">
     Next Page
   </button></td></tr></table></center>
<h3>(JS) Arrays</h3>
<blockquote><blockquote><blockquote>
<p>
Arrays are special objects in they hold many different values within a single variable. Very useful if you want
to perform the same action or method against many values within the array. We create arrays using
the <b>new</b><u>Keyword</u> Array(7);. this will create a new array with 7 items in

the array.
to add values to the array we use square brackets [ ] and we add the position inside the brackets
like
<i><script>
var array new Array(7);
a[0] = "Bear"; (first position begins with zero).
a[1] = "Elk"; (next first position from zero).
a[2] = "Bobcat"; (third value from beginning).
a[3] = "Mountain Lion"; (first position begins with zero).
a[4] = 90; (note you can enter numbers).
a[5] = "deer"; (if you fail to use quotes the string will be converted to a number and fail to run).
a[6] = true; (boolean words true and false or reserved as special value).
document.write(newline);
document.write(a[0] + coma +a[1] + coma +a[2] + coma +a[3] + coma +a[4] + coma +a[5] + coma +a[6]);
</script></i>
See how we can mix variable values and test against the various values if we wish.
</p>
<script>
var newline = "<br>";
var coma = ", ";
var arr = "Array has the following ";
var a = new Array(7);
a[0] = "Bear"; //(first position begins with zero).
a[1] = "Elk"; // (next first position from zero).
a[2] = "Bobcat"; //(third value from beginning).
a[3] = "Mountain Lion"; // (first position begins with zero).
a[4] = 90; // (note you can enter numbers).
a[5] = "deer";// (if you fail to use quotes the string will be converted to a number).
a[6] = true; //(boolean words true and false or reserved as special value).
document.write(arr);
document.write(newline);
document.write(a[0] + coma +a[1] + coma +a[2] + coma +a[3] + coma +a[4] + coma +a[5] + coma +a[6]);
</script>
<p>
Arrays can also be built using the following var b = new Array ("Moose", "Grouse", true, 20);
And they also can be built not using new key word like this var c = ["Antelop", "Buffalo", false, 17];
Outputing to the webpage is done the same by document.write(c[1]); would give you Buffalo.
</p>

Arrays

Array can hold many values of different types using a box index [0], index [1], index [2] and so forth.
 Values for each indexed [ ] is entered all on one line like this below
var tomSmith = ["Tom Smith", "123 Quaker St.", 120.50];
 write to the screen like "1st Index value is = ", tomSmith[0], and so forth.


```
<script>
document.write("Creating an Array using [] brackets " + "<br />");
var tomSmith = ["Tom Smith", "123 Quaker St.", 120.50];
document.write("Displaying the values for each index " + "<br />");
document.write("1st Index value is = ", tomSmith[0], "<br />");
document.write("2nd Index value is = ", tomSmith[1], "<br />");
document.write("3rd Index value is = ", tomSmith[2], "<br />");
document.write("Knowing the last index we can add simply by tomSmith[3] = value " +
"<br />");
tomSmith[3] = "tSmith@aol.com";
document.write("3rd Index value is = ", tomSmith[3], "<br />");
document.write("Displaying the added values for each index " ,tomSmith , "<br />");
document.write("We can replace a value via splice " + "<br />");
tomSmith.splice(2, 1, "Pittsburgh", "PA");
document.write("Displaying the replaced values for each index " ,tomSmith , "<br />");
document.write("We can remove any index and value via splice as well meaning start at
four and remove only in that one location " + "<br />");
tomSmith.splice(4,1);
document.write("Displaying after removal of values for 4th index " ,tomSmith , "<br />");
document.write("Array to string : ", tomSmith.valueOf(), "<br />");
document.write("Array to string comma seperated : ", tomSmith.join(", "), "<br />");
document.write("Array to string : ", tomSmith.toString(), "<br />");
document.write("Array to string underscore seperated : ", tomSmith.join("_"), "<br />");
delete tomSmith[3];
document.write("Displaying after removal of values for 3rd index " ,tomSmith , "<br />");
tomSmith.sort();
document.write("Displaying after sorting " ,tomSmith , "<br />");
tomSmith.reverse();
document.write("Displaying after reverse sorting " ,tomSmith , "<br />");
var numbers = [4,3,9,1,20, 43];
document.write("Array of numbers " ,numbers , "<br />");
numbers.sort(function (x,y){ return x-y});
document.write("Displaying sorting of numbers lowest to highest x-y " ,numbers , "<br
/>");
numbers.sort(function (x,y){ return y-x});
document.write("Displaying sorting of numbers highest to lowest y-x " ,numbers , "<br
/>");
document.write("Array to string : ", numbers.toString(), "<br />");
var combinedArray = numbers.concat(tomSmith);
document.write(" Combined Array using concat : ", combinedArray, "<br />");
```

```
tomSmith.pop();
document.write("Displaying after removing end " ,tomSmith ,  "<br />");
tomSmith.push("555-231-1212", "US");
document.write("Displaying after adding to end " ,tomSmith ,  "<br />");
tomSmith.shift();
tomSmith.shift();
document.write("Displaying after removing 1st index " ,tomSmith ,  "<br />");
tomSmith.unshift("Thomas Smith");
document.write("Displaying after adding new 1st index " ,tomSmith ,  "<br />");
document.write("Displaying using for loop " , "<br />");
for (i = 0; i <tomSmith.length; i++){
document.write(tomSmith[i] ,  "<br />");
}
</script>
<h2>toString()</h2>
<p>The toString() method returns an array as a comma separated string:</p>

<p id="demo"></p>
<p> script command statements: <br>
const fruits = ["Banana", "Orange", "Apple", "Mango"];<br>
document.getElementById("demo").innerHTML = fruits.toString();<br></p>
<script>
const fruits = ["Banana", "Orange", "Apple", "Mango"];
document.getElementById("demo").innerHTML = fruits.toString();
</script>
<p>The join() method joins array elements into a string.</p>
<p>It this example we have used " * " as a separator between the elements:</p>

<p id="demo1"></p>
<p id="demo2"></p>
<script>
const fruit = ["Banana", "Orange", "Apple", "Mango"];
document.getElementById("demo1").innerHTML = fruit.join(" * ");
document.getElementById("demo2").innerHTML = fruit;
</script>
<p> script command statements: <br>
const fruit = ["Banana", "Orange", "Apple", "Mango"];<br>
document.getElementById("demo1").innerHTML = fruit.join(" * ");<br>
document.getElementById("demo2").innerHTML = fruit;</p>

<p>The pop() method removes the last element from an array.</p>
<p> script command statements: <br>
const fruite = ["Banana", "Orange", "Apple", "Mango"];<br>
document.getElementById("demo3").innerHTML = fruite;
fruite.pop();<br>
document.getElementById("demo4").innerHTML = fruite;</p>
```

```
<p id="demo3"></p>
<p id="demo4"></p>
<script>
const fruite = ["Banana", "Orange", "Apple", "Mango"];
document.getElementById("demo3").innerHTML = fruite;
fruite.pop();
document.getElementById("demo4").innerHTML = fruite;
</script>
```
<p>The pop() method in the print statement prints the item removed as the last element from an array. Then displays array.</p>
<p> script command statements:
const fruita = ["Banana", "Orange", "Apple", "Kiwi"];
document.getElementById("demo5").innerHTML = fruita.pop();
fruite.pop();
document.getElementById("demo4").innerHTML = fruita;</p>
<p id="demo5"></p>
<p id="demo6"></p>
```
<script>
const fruita = ["Banana", "Orange", "Apple", "Kiwi"];
document.getElementById("demo5").innerHTML = fruita.pop();
document.getElementById("demo6").innerHTML = fruita;
</script>
```

 Comma separated values or CSV files are just a text file named with extention .csv but they are earliest form of spreadsheets.
However they can be read as an array within an array. The bigger primary array holds the row numbers from row[0] to row[xxxxxxxxetc]
and the inner array holds the values separated with commas. These can be displayed in a HTML table like this <a href=csv_table_display.html> Display CSV as Table</a> by looping with a "for loop".
<script type="text/javascript">
   function Upload() {
      var fileUpload = document.getElementById("fileUpload");
      var regex = /^([a-zA-Z0-9\s_\\.\-:])+(.csv|.txt)$/;
      if (regex.test(fileUpload.value.toLowerCase())) {
       if (typeof (FileReader) != "undefined") {
         var reader = new FileReader();
         reader.onload = function (e) {
           var table = document.createElement("table");
           var rows = e.target.result.split("\n");
           for (var i = 0; i < rows.length; i++) {
             var row = table.insertRow(-1);
             var cells = rows[i].split(",");
             for (var j = 0; j < cells.length; j++) {
               var cell = row.insertCell(-1);
               cell.innerHTML = cells[j];
             }

```
                    }<br>
                    var dvCSV = document.getElementById("dvCSV");<br>
                    dvCSV.innerHTML = "";<br>
                    dvCSV.appendChild(table);<br>
                }<br>
                reader.readAsText(fileUpload.files[0]);<br>
            } else {<br>
                alert("This browser does not support HTML5.");<br>
            }<br>
        } else {<br>
            alert("Please upload a valid CSV file.");<br>
        }<br>
    }<br>
&lt;/script&gt;<br>
&lt;input type="file" style="background-color:orange" id="fileUpload" /&gt;<br>
&lt;input type="button" style="background-color:lightgreen" id="upload" value="Upload"
onclick="Upload()" /&gt;<br>
&lt;hr /&gt;<br>
&lt;div id="dvCSV"&gt;<br>
&lt;/div&gt; <br>
<br>
```

There are two "for loops" one inside of the other that collect the information to put a value within a table data tag. Building the row and columns
That are then appended to the table at the end of each row. Do a mental walk through and tell yourself why and where it displays it on the page?
</blockquote></blockquote></blockquote>

```
 <center><table><tr><td>     </td><td><button
class="HB"
   onclick="window.location.href = 'site_menu.html';">
     Site Menu
</button></td><td>     </td><td><button class="HB"
   onclick="window.location.href = 'lindex.html';">
     Begin Lessons
   </button></td><td>     </td><td><button class="HB"
   onclick="window.location.href = 'pageL5.html';">
     Last Page
   </button></td><td>     </td><td><button class="HB"
   onclick="window.location.href = 'pageL7.html';">
     Next Page
   </button></td></tr></table></center>
```

```
</body>
</html>
```

****

pageL7.html
****

```html
<!DOCTYPE html>
<html lang="en">
<head>
<meta charset="utf-8">
<title>Page 7</title>
<style>//CSS goes here</style>
<SCRIPT LANGUAGE="JavaScript">
// javascript functions go here or in body
</SCRIPT>
</head>
<body>
<h3>(JS) Javascript DOD HandBook</h3>
<h4>How to code without coding tools Page 7</h4>
 <center><table><tr><td>     </td><td><button
class="HB"
   onclick="window.location.href = 'site_menu.html';">
     Site Menu
</button></td><td>     </td><td><button class="HB"
   onclick="window.location.href = 'lindex.html';">
     Begin Lessons
  </button></td><td>     </td><td><button class="HB"
   onclick="window.location.href = 'pageL6.html';">
     Last Page
   </button></td><td>     </td><td><button class="HB"
   onclick="window.location.href = 'pageL8.html';">
     Next Page
   </button></td></tr></table></center>
<h3>(JS) FUNCTIONS</h3>
<blockquote><blockquote><blockquote>
<p><h3>Functions</h3>
<p>
Functions are reuseable code, used or called, any where as many times as you would
like. These are built <br>
by using function keyword name of the <b>function() using curly brackets { //code;  }
</b>like this  <br>
<i>&lt;script&gt;  <br>
function sayHello(){ <br>
document.write("Hello Pioneer"); <br>
} <br>
&lt;/script&gt; </i> <br>
```

For example:

<script>
function sayHello(){
document.write("Hello Pioneer");
}
sayHello();
var newline = "<br>";
document.write(newline);
</script>

We can call or <i>invoke</i> this function by entering sayHello(); in the script tags. Or
create a <i>trigger event</i>
within the HTML page to call the function "on click" in a form.
We can also declare a variable within the function then give that variable a value when
we call the function.
like
<i><script>
function sayHay(who){
document.write("Hello Pilgrim" + who);
}

sayHay("Tage");
</script> </i>
<script>
function sayHay(who){
document.write("Hello Pilgrim" + who);
}
sayHay("Tage");
</script>
</p>
Plus we can change the who input like sayHay("alice"); and the hello message.
<script>
function sayHey(who){
document.write("Hello Padowan " + who);
}
sayHey("Tage");
var newline = "<br>";
document.write(newline);
sayHey("Alice");
var newline = "<br>";
document.write(newline);
</script>
<i><script>
function sayHey(who){
document.write("Hello Padowan " + who);
}
sayHey("Tage");

```
var newline = "&lt;br&gt;";<br>
document.write(newline);<br>
sayHey("Alice");<br>
var newline = "&lt;br&gt;";<br>
document.write(newline);<br>
&lt;script&gt;</i><br>
```
<h3>Functions Overview</h3>
Functions are containerized and reuseable code.

```
<script>
document.write("A function to check for a value in any array " + "<br />");
function inArray(arrayToCheck, value){
for(i =  0; arrayToCheck.length; i++){
if ( arrayToCheck[i] === value){
return true;
}
}
return false;
}
var randArray = [1, 2, 3, 4, 5, 6, 7, 8, 9];
document.write("In randArray looking for a value  4 ", inArray(randArray, 4), "<br />");
var timArray = ["tom", "dick", "harry", "peter", "paul", "mary"];
document.write("In timArray looking for a value  mary ", inArray(timArray, "mary"), "<br
/>");
document.write("In randArray looking for a value  9 ", inArray(randArray, 9), "<br />");

document.write("Demonstrating a local variable " + "<br />");

</script>
```
A local variable is one that remains within the function and is not available outside to the
function. Consider the following block of code.

```
function times2(num){<br>
var var2= 2;<br>
return num * var2;<br>
document.write("var 2 is =  " ,var2,  "&lt;br /&gt;"); // this will send output to the screen or
```
webpage but the outside will not

```
}
//document.write("var 2 is =  " ,var2,  "&lt;br /&gt;"); <br>
document.write("var2 is local variable inside the function and is not available outside of
```
the function " + "<br />");

```
<script>
document.write("var2 testing " + "<br />");
function times2(num){
var var2 = 2;
return num * var2;
document.write("var2 testing " + "<br />");
document.write("<br>var 2 is =  " ,var2,  "<br />");
```

```
}
//document.write("var 2 is = " ,var2,  "<br />"); // this will not run at all in the DOD SDC
document.write("var2 is local variable inside the function and is not available outside of
the function " +  "<br />");
</script>
<br>But if we take this same code and pass it as variable to another function it will run
okay. <br>
function times2(num){<br>
var var2 = 2;<br>
return num * var2;<br>
}<br>
function times3(num){<br>
return num * 3;<br>
}<br>
function multiply (func, num){<br>
return func(num);<br>
}<br>
document.write("3 * 15 = ", multiply(times2, 15), "&lt;br /&gt;");<br>
And likewise times3 function.<br>
<script>
function times2(num){
var var2 = 2;
return num * var2;
}
function times3(num){
return num * 3;
}
function multiply (func, num){
return func(num);
}
document.write("3 * 15 = ", multiply(times2, 15), "<br />");
document.write("3 * 15 = ", multiply(times3, 15), "<br />");
</script>
You can also use function expressions.<br>
<script>
var triple = function(num){
return num * 3;
}
document.write("3 * 45 = ", multiply(triple, 45), "<br />");
</script>
A function get the sum of the numbers given to the function. <br>
<script>
function getSum(){
var sum = 0;
for (i=0; i < arguments.length; i++){
sum += arguments[i];
```

```
}
return sum;
}
document.write("Sum = ", getSum(1, 2, 3, 4, 5, 6), "<br />");
</script>
```
A function to create a new array of numbers and times each array value by 2.

```
<script>
function times2(theArray){
var newArray = [];
for (i =0; i < theArray.length; i++){
  newArray.push(theArray[i] * 2);
}
return newArray;
}
document.write("Array Doubled = ", times2([1, 2, 3, 4, 5, 6]).toString(), "<br />");
</script>
```
Functions that call themselves is known as recursive function and below demonstrates this.

```
<script>
function factorial(num){
if(num <= 1){
return 1;
} else {
return num * factorial(num-1);
}
}
document.write("Factorial of 4 = ", factorial(4), "<br />");

</script>
// 1st: num = 4 * factorial(3) = 4 * 6 = 24<br>
// 2nd: num = 3 * factorial(2) = 3 * 2 = 6<br>
// 3rd: num = 2 * factorial(1) = 1 * 2 = 2<br>
```
this passes first time the 4 factorial(num-1) = 4-1 = 3
2nd pass is 3 factorial(num-1) = 3 -1 = 2
3rd pass is 2 factorial(num-1) = 2-1 = 1
it tries once more 4th pass is 1 factorial(num-1) = 1-1 = 0
but the if said less than or = 1 and zero is less than
executes the code return1; meaning it will return to start of 4 1*2 then 2*3 then 4*6
the way out when there is no more values to calculate.

Four functions and 4 buttons "trigger events examples" with different results.

```
<p id=demo> </p>
<p id=demo0> </p>
<p id=demo1> </p>
<p id=demo3> </p>
<p id=demo4> </p>
```

```html
<p id=demo5> </p>
<p id=demo6> </p>
<p id=demo7> </p>
<p id=demo8> </p>
<script>
function msg(){
alert("hello! This is the message");
}
document.getElementById("demo0").innerHTML = " Click  button to see responses ";
var see = "<br>Writing to the webpage."
function msg1(){
document.getElementById("demo").innerHTML = see + "  - This is value of - Writing to
the webpage - in the variable with the trigger event of clicking - write to webpage -
button.";
}
var see1 = "Adding another message to the screen."
function msg2(){
document.getElementById("demo1").innerHTML = see1 + "  - This is value of a
different variable. Written to webpage.";
}
function getcube(number){
alert(number*number*number);
}
</script>

<script>
document.write(getInfo());
//document.getElementById("demo3").innerHTML = "  <br> Cool or What!";
//document.getElementById("demo4").innerHTML = "  <br> Are you paying attention
where it writes out the messages verses when it was called?";
</script>

<form>
<input type="button" onclick="msg()" value="call function"/>
<input type="button" onclick="msg1()" value="write to webpage"/>
<input type="button" onclick="msg2()" value="Button is the trigger event"/>
<input type="button" onclick="getcube(4)" value="Click to get the cube of 4 - (4X4X4),
passed argument in getcube(4) to script" />
</form>

</blockquote></blockquote></blockquote>
 <center><table><tr><td>     </td><td><button
class="HB"
    onclick="window.location.href = 'site_menu.html';">
      Site Menu
</button></td><td>     </td><td><button class="HB"
```

```
onclick="window.location.href = 'lindex.html';">
    Begin Lessons
</button></td><td>     </td><td><button class="HB"
onclick="window.location.href = 'pageL6.html';">
    Last Page
</button></td><td>     </td><td><button class="HB"
onclick="window.location.href = 'pageL8.html';">
    Next Page
</button></td></tr></table></center>

<p style="color:lightgray">
Public Domain copywrite &copy; version 0 - Author retains rights to any additional
versions or editions<br>
Author: Brent Lichfield
</p>
</body>
</html>
```

```
*******************************
pageL8.html
*******************************
<!DOCTYPE html>
<html lang="en">
<head>
<meta charset="utf-8">
<title>Page 8</title>
<style>//CSS goes here</style>
<SCRIPT LANGUAGE="JavaScript">
// javascript functions go here or in body
</SCRIPT>
</head>
<body onload='document.form1.text1.focus()'>
<h3>(JS) Javascript DOD HandBook</h3>
<h4>How to code without coding tools Page 8</h4>
 <center><table><tr><td>     </td><td><button
class="HB"
   onclick="window.location.href = 'site_menu.html';">
    Site Menu
</button></td><td>     </td><td><button class="HB"
   onclick="window.location.href = 'lindex.html';">
    Begin Lessons
</button></td><td>     </td><td><button class="HB"
   onclick="window.location.href = 'pageL7.html';">
    Last Page
</button></td><td>     </td><td><button class="HB"
   onclick="window.location.href = 'pageL9.html';">
```

Next Page
```
</button></td></tr></table></center>
<h3>(JS) FORM VALIDATIONS</h3>
<blockquote><blockquote><blockquote>
<p>There are several ways to do form validations. Normally the Javascript would stay
on the page with a form action="#"<br>
and the values submitted would just be available for testing in a function or statement.
More commonly after the values<br>
had been validated by Javascript the results would have been put in a string and
shipped across the internet to a webserver.<br>
The Webserver would use some other programing language to extract the passed string
and use it to return a webpage<br>
for display to the user. A little known but useful for this training is to pass the form
values to another webpage on the training site.<br>
This webpage then can extract the name=value pairs and display them as write
statements. Basically echoing the inputs<br>
passed. The form validations are done before passing the values to the other webpage.
</p>
<p>The following is a simple request for email that will remain on the page giving a
result in an alert box. <br></p>
<h2>Input an email and Submit</h2>
<form name="form1" action="#">
<ul>
<li><input type='text' name='text1'/></li>
<li> </li>
<li class="submit"><input type="submit" name="submit" value="Submit"
onclick="ValidateEmail(document.form1.text1)"/></li>
<li> </li>
</ul>
</form>
</div>
<script >
function ValidateEmail(inputText)
{
var mailformat = /^\w+([\.-]?\w+)*@\w+([\.-]?\w+)*(\.\w{2,3})+$/;
if(inputText.value.match(mailformat))
{
alert("Valid email address!");
document.form1.text1.focus();
return true;
}
else
{
alert("You have entered an invalid email address!");
document.form1.text1.focus();
return false;
```

```
}
}
```
</script>
<p>What makes this work is when the body onload='document.form1.text1.focus()' is loaded it also calls a function.
Then a form is loaded using a html list to display it on the screen. This becomes the input for the function as arguements
<form name="form1" action="#">
<ul>
<li><input type='text' name='text1'/></li>
<li> </li>
<li class="submit"><input type="submit" name="submit" value="Submit" onclick="ValidateEmail(document.form1.text1)"/></li>
<li> </li>
</ul>
</form>

Note that the action to form is "#" meaning do not process beyond this webpage. Then input text is matched to a mailformat
this mailformat is a <b> regex or reqular expression </b>asking that certain things be included in the email like a @ and . dot something ending.
Regex for the mail is
var mailformat = /^\w+([\.-]?\w+)*@\w+([\.-]?\w+)*(\.\w{2,3})+$/;
Regex for letters only
var letters = /^[A-Za-z]+$/;
Regex for numbers only
var numbers = /^[0-9]+$/;
Regex for date
 var dateformat = /^(0?[1-9]|1[012])[\/\-](0?[1-9]|[12][0-9]|3[01])[\/\-]\d{4}$/;
Regex for password having 7 minimum characters and 15 maximum characters
var paswd= /^(?=.*[0-9])(?=.*[!@#$%^&*])[a-zA-Z0-9!@#$%^&*]{7,15}$/;
Regex for phone number having two hypens in correct locations like 801-771-0390
var phoneno = /^\(?([0-9]{3})\)?[-.]?([0-9]{3})[-.]?([0-9]{4})$/;
Regex for numbers only credit card
var creditCard = /^\(?([0-9]{4})\)?[-.]?([0-9]{4})[-.]?([0-9]{4})$/;
<script>
function ValidateEmail(inputText)
{
var mailformat = /^\w+([\.-]?\w+)*@\w+([\.-]?\w+)*(\.\w{2,3})+$/;
if(inputText.value.match(mailformat))
{
alert("Valid email address!");
document.form1.text1.focus();
return true;
}
else

{
alert("You have entered an invalid email address!");
document.form1.text1.focus();
return false;
}
}
</script>
</p>
<p>The following is a simple registration form that will send inputs to a echoing webpage.
</p>
<p id="paragraph"></p>
<form action=formnext1.html>
  <input id="choose" name="i-like" placeholder="Enter user-id" required />
<input type="email" placeholder="email@example.io" id="email" name=email required />
<input type="password" placeholder="Enter your password" id="password" name=passwrd required />
<input type="password" placeholder="Re-Enter your password" id="confirm-password" name=ids required />
<label for="male">Male</label>
<input type="radio" id="male" name="gender" value="male" />
<label for="female">Female</label>
<input type="radio" id="female" name="gender" value="female" />
<label for="others">Others</label>
<input type="radio" id="others" name="gender" value="others" />
<select id="title" name=title required>
  <option value="">Select One Title</option>
  <option value="Mr">Mr</option>
  <option value="Mrs">Mrs</option>
  <option value="Ms">Ms</option>
</select>
<input type="checkbox" id="terms" name=terms>
<label for="terms">I agree to the terms and conditions</label>

 <button>Submit</button>
<form>
The following is the script that makes each validation check and the form action directs it to another webpage.
<script>
    const paragraph = document.getElementById('parapgraph');
    paragraph.innerText = 'This is a paragraph tag';

const emailInput = document.getElementById('email');
const emailRegex = /^[a-zA-Z0-9.!#$%&'*+/=?^_`{|}~-]+@[a-zA-Z0-9-]+(?:\.[a-zA-Z0-9-]+)*$/;
if (!emailInput.value.match(emailRegex)) {
  alert('Invalid email address.');

```
}<br>

const password = document.getElementById('password').value;<br>
const confirmPassword = document.getElementById('confirm-password').value;<br>
if (password.value !== confirmPassword.value) {<br>
  alert('Entered passwords do not match');<br>
}<br>
if (password.length < 6) {<br>
  alert('Password must be more than 6 characters long')<br>
}<br>

const genders = document.getElementsByName("gender");<br>
const validForm = false;<br>
let i = 0;<br>
while (!validForm && i < radios.length) {<br>
  if (radios[i].checked) validForm = true;<br>
  i++;  <br>
}<br>
if (!validForm) alert("Must check some option!");<br>

const title = document.getElementById('title');<br>
if (title.value = "") {<br>
  alert('Please select a title');<br>
}<br>

const terms = document.getElementById('terms');<br>
if (!terms.checked) {<br>
  alert('Please agree to the terms and conditions to proceed further.');<br>
}<br>
  &lt;/script&gt;<br>
<script>
    const paragraph = document.getElementById('parapgraph');
    paragraph.innerText = 'This is a paragraph tag';

const emailInput = document.getElementById('email');
const emailRegex = /^[a-zA-Z0-9.!#$%&'*+/=?^_`{|}~-]+@[a-zA-Z0-9-]+(?:\.[a-zA-Z0-9-]+)*$/;
if (!emailInput.value.match(emailRegex)) {
  alert('Invalid email address.');
}

const password = document.getElementById('password').value;
const confirmPassword = document.getElementById('confirm-password').value;
if (password.value !== confirmPassword.value) {
  alert('Entered passwords do not match');
}
```

```
if (password.length < 6) {
  alert('Password must be more than 6 characters long')
}

const genders = document.getElementsByName("gender");
const validForm = false;
let i = 0;
while (!validForm && i < radios.length) {
  if (radios[i].checked) validForm = true;
  i++;
}
if (!validForm) alert("Must check some option!");

const title = document.getElementById('title');
if (title.value = "") {
  alert('Please select a title');
}

const terms = document.getElementById('terms');
if (!terms.checked) {
  alert('Please agree to the terms and conditions to proceed further.');
}
  </script>
</p>
```

```html
</blockquote></blockquote></blockquote>
 <center><table><tr><td>     </td><td><button
class="HB"
   onclick="window.location.href = 'site_menu.html';">
     Site Menu
</button></td><td>     </td><td><button class="HB"
   onclick="window.location.href = 'lindex.html';">
     Begin Lessons
  </button></td><td>     </td><td><button class="HB"
   onclick="window.location.href = 'pageL7.html';">
     Last Page
  </button></td><td>     </td><td><button class="HB"
   onclick="window.location.href = 'pageL9.html';">
     Next Page
  </button></td></tr></table></center>

<p style="color:lightgray">
Public Domain copywrite &copy; version 0 - Author retains rights to any additional
versions or editions<br>
Author: Brent Lichfield
</p>
```

```
</body>
</html>
```

```
<!DOCTYPE html>
<html lang="en">
<head>
<meta charset="utf-8">
<title>Page 9</title>
<style>//CSS goes here</style>
<SCRIPT LANGUAGE="JavaScript">
// javascript functions go here or in body
</SCRIPT>
</head>
<body>
<h3>(JS) Javascript DOD HandBook</h3>
<h4>How to code without coding tools Page 9</h4>
 <center><table><tr><td>     </td><td><button
class="HB"
   onclick="window.location.href = 'site_menu.html';">
     Site Menu
</button></td><td>     </td><td><button class="HB"
   onclick="window.location.href = 'lindex.html';">
     Begin Lessons
  </button></td><td>     </td><td><button class="HB"
   onclick="window.location.href = 'pageL8.html';">
     Last Page
  </button></td><td>     </td><td><button class="HB"
   onclick="window.location.href = 'pageL10.html';">
     Next Page
  </button></td></tr></table></center>
<h3>(JS) CONDITIONALS & FLOW CONTROL</h3>
<p><blockquote><blockquote><blockquote><br><u>Conditionals</u> are used to
determine a choice and the block of code that goes with each one.<br> Providing an
outcome or consequence of choice kind of like real life.<br><br>
Relational Operators: == != > < >= <=  (== is equal to but normally we use === to be
exactly equal to. != is not equal to and <br>
== is equal to value either number or string but === is equal to but also equal to type of
variable must match as well number = number<br>
(see below 5 is or is not equal to 5). > is greater than  while <  is less than. >= is greater
that or equal to and <= is less than or equal to.) <br>
Logical Operators: && || ! . (&& is AND, || is OR, and ! is not preceding one of the other
logicals.<br> <br>
<script>
```

```
document.write("true || false  both are equal to = ",true || false ,"<br>");
document.write("!true != to true = ", !true ,"<br>");
document.write("\"5\" == 5 = ",("5" == 5) ,"<br>");
document.write("\"5\" === 5 != ",("5" === 5) ,"<br>");
</script><br>
```

<u>IF statements</u> used to test a condition like person's age and can he or she go to school. if ((age >= 1) && (age < 5)) {
document.write("Go to Preschool") An else if is alternate condition like else if ((age>= 5) && (age <= 6)) {document.write("Go to Kindergarten" and usually should have a default condition if nothing tested matches. else { document.write("Go to Grade",}
&lt:script>

```
var age = 8;<br>
document.write("Person's age is ",age ,"&lt;br /&gt;");<br>
if ((age  >= 1) && (age < 5)) {<br>
document.write("Go to Preschool" + "&lt;br /&gt;");<br>
}<br>
else if ((age>= 5) && (age <= 6)) {<br>
document.write("Go to Kindergarten" + "&lt;br /&gt;");<br>
} else if (age > 18){<br>
document.write("Go to College or trade school" + "&lt;br /&gt;");<br>
} else {<br>
document.write("Go to Grade", age -5 ,"&lt;br /&gt;");<br>
}<br>
```
&lt:/script>
 if age is set to 8 the result is below


```
<script>

var age = 8;
document.write("Person's age is ",age ,"<br>");
if ((age  >= 1) && (age < 5)) {
document.write("Go to Preschool" + "<br />");
}
else if ((age>= 5) && (age <= 6)) {
document.write("Go to Kindergarten" + "<br />");
} else if (age > 18){
document.write("Go to College or trade school" + "<br />");
} else {
document.write("Go to Grade", age -5 ,"<br />");
}
</script><br>
```
<u>Switch case statements:</u> used when the test or options results are low. Like var age = 5;
```
switch (age) {
case 3:
case 4:
case 5:
```

```
document.write("Go to Kindergarten" );
break;<br>
```
When a case is true then a keyword break stops the execution and running of the code block.


```
<script>
var age1 = 25;
document.write(age1 + "<br />");
switch (age1) {
case 3:
case 4:
case 5:
document.write("Go to Kindergarten" + "<br />");
break;
case 6:
document.write("Go to Grade", age1 -5 ," public school <br />");
break;
case 7:
default:
document.write("Go Professional Student be a doctor or such ", age1 -5 ," never quit learning <br />");
}
</script>
<script>
var age = 5;
document.write(" OOPS mistake on application form you are only " + age + "<br />");
switch (age) {
case 3:
case 4:
case 5:
document.write("Go to Kindergarten" + "<br />");
break;
case 6:
document.write("Go to Grade", age -5 ," public school <br />");
break;
default:
document.write("Go to Grade", age -5 ," never quit learning <br />");
}
</script>
```
Above code inside the script tags
<script>
var age = 5;
document.write(" OOPS mistake on application form you are only " + age + "<br />");
switch (age) {
case 3:
case 4:

case 5:
document.write("Go to Kindergarten" + "<br />");
break;
case 6:
document.write("Go to Grade", age -5 ," public school
");
break;
default:
document.write("Go to Grade", age -5 ," never quit learning
");
}
</script>

<u>Ternary Operators</u> is used when there are but two outcomes.Like var age =
25;var canIVote = (age >= 18) ? true : false;

<script>
var age = 25;
var canIVote = (age >= 18) ? true : false;
document.write("Can you Vote? True or False your age is ", age, " Your status is ",
canIVote , "
");

</script>
<script>
var age = 25;
var canIVote = (age >= 18) ? true : false;
document.write("Can you Vote? True or False your age is ", age, " Your status is ",
canIVote , "
");

</script>
In switch statements you can use the keyword return instead of break to rerun
through the block of code. And you can use
you can use the keyword continue to skip the next line in a block code.
</blockquote></blockquote></blockquote>
 <table><tr><td>   </td><td><button
class="HB"
   onclick="window.location.href = 'site_menu.html';">
     Site Menu
</button></td><td>   </td><td><button class="HB"
   onclick="window.location.href = 'lindex.html';">
     Begin Lessons
   </button></td><td>   </td><td><button class="HB"
   onclick="window.location.href = 'pageL8.html';">
     Last Page
   </button></td><td>   </td><td><button class="HB"
   onclick="window.location.href = 'pageL10.html';">
     Next Page
   </button></td></tr></table>

</p>
</body>
</html>

****
pageL10.html
****

```
<!DOCTYPE html>
<html lang="en">
<head>
<meta charset="utf-8">
<title>Page 10</title>
<style>//CSS goes here</style>
<SCRIPT LANGUAGE="JavaScript">
// javascript functions go here or in body
</SCRIPT>
</head>
<body>
<h3>(JS) Javascript DOD HandBook</h3>
<h4>How to code without coding tools Page 10</h4>
 <center><table><tr><td>     </td><td><button
class="HB"
   onclick="window.location.href = 'site_menu.html';">
     Site Menu
</button></td><td>     </td><td><button class="HB"
   onclick="window.location.href = 'lindex.html';">
     Begin Lessons
  </button></td><td>     </td><td><button class="HB"
   onclick="window.location.href = 'pageL9.html';">
     Last Page
  </button></td><td>     </td><td><button class="HB"
   onclick="window.location.href = 'pageL11.html';">
     Next Page
  </button></td></tr></table></center>
<h3>(JS)LOOPS</h3>
<blockquote><blockquote><blockquote>
<u>Loops</u> are used when you want to perform something repeatatively. Like 10
times. var i = 1;while(i <= 10){document.write(i ); i++;}
<br>Beware of infinite loops created by not having a limit to how many times the block
of code is run. <br><br>
<script>
document.write("While Loop ", "<br>");
document.write("i is used as a incrementor the while is until <= 10 ", "<br>");
```

```
var i = 1;
while(i <= 10){
document.write(i +"<br>");
i++;
}
</script><br>
```
Decision LOOPS such as **for of, for in, for each, while loops** are used to perform same or similar blocks of code
for each arguement or until a specified condition is met.
<script>
        document.write("Do While Loop performs the while until condition is met like a guessing game", "<br>");
//document.write("i is used as a incrementor the while is until <= 10 ", "<br>");
do{ var guess = prompt ("Guess a number between 1 and 20 or 15 to bypass");}
while(guess != 15) alert ("You guessed the right number it was 15!")
</script>

```
<script>
document.write("Do While Loop  performs the while until condition is met like a guessing
game", "<br>");
//document.write("i is used as a incrementor the while is until <= 10 ", "<br>");
do{ var guess = prompt ("Guess a number between 1 and 20 or 15 to bypass");}
while(guess != 15) alert ("You guessed the right number it was 15!")
</script><br>
```
<u>For</u> loops are self contained meaning instead of having values declared outside of it like a while loop all the values are withing the loop.

```
<script>
document.write("for(j = 0; j <= 20; j++){// perform until 20 is met}","<br>");
document.write(" if ((j % 2) === 0) if j is modulus by 2 then it will equal zero or a test for
even numbers","<br>");
document.write(" continue keyword stops execution returns to the for loop just before
incrementing j","<br>");
document.write(" break keyword stops execution of entire loop and executes statement
below the loop","<br>");
document.write(" if (j === 15){break} will stop the printing of j after odd numbers 13
","<br>");
for(j = 0; j <= 20; j++){
if ((j % 2) === 0) {
continue;
}
if (j === 15){
break;
}
document.write(j +"<br>");
}
document.write("End of the for loop","<br>");
</script><br>
```
<script>

document.write("for(j = 0; j <= 20; j++){// perform until 20 is met}","<br>");
document.write(" if ((j % 2) === 0) if j is modulus by 2 then it will equal zero or a test for
even numbers","<br>");
document.write(" continue keyword stops execution returns to the for loop just before
incrementing j","<br>");
document.write(" break keyword stops execution of entire loop and executes statement
below the loop","<br>");
document.write(" if (j === 15){break} will stop the printing of j after odd numbers 13
","<br>");
for(j = 0; j <= 20; j++){
if ((j % 2) === 0) {
continue;
}
if (j === 15){
break;
}
document.write(j +"<br>");
}
document.write("End of the for loop","<br>");
</script>
Exercise: what does the break and "continue" in the for loop really
do? Add comments and save.

<u>For in</u> loop: used with objects more of that in the objects lessons.var customer
= {name : "Bob Thomas", address : "123 Main Street", balance : $50.50 } for (k in
customer){document.write(customer[k] + "<br>");}
<script>
//document.write("
begin of the for in loop","<br>");
var customer = {name : "Bob Thomas", address : "123 Main Street", balance : 50.50 };
//document.write("
begin of the for in loop","<br>");
for (k in customer){
document.write(customer[k] + "<br />");
}
</script>
(Example of troubleshooting). I used this to start with :var customer = {name ; ""Bob
Thomas", address : "123 Main Street", balance : $50.50 } for (k in
customer){document.write(customer[k] + "<br>");} But what happened is nothing
would print out to the page. To diagnose the problem I added this line document.write("

begin of the for in loop","<br>"); and worked through the code block one
line at time then used // to comment out the line to determine where my problem was.
Errors found ""Bob to many quotes and name; should have been name: and no ; ending
the command statement.
var customer = {name : "Bob Thomas", address : "123
Main Street", balance : 50.50 }; is the corrections.

</blockquote></blockquote></blockquote>
 <center><table><tr><td>   </td><td><button

```
class="HB"
   onclick="window.location.href = 'site_menu.html';">
      Site Menu
</button></td><td>     </td><td><button class="HB"
   onclick="window.location.href = 'lindex.html';">
      Begin Lessons
   </button></td><td>     </td><td><button class="HB"
   onclick="window.location.href = 'pageL9.html';">
      Last Page
   </button></td><td>     </td><td><button class="HB"
   onclick="window.location.href = 'pageL11.html';">
      Next Page
   </button></td></tr></table></center>

<p style="color:lightgray">
Public Domain copywrite &copy; version 0 - Author retains rights to any additional
versions or editions<br>
Author: Brent Lichfield
</p>
</body>
</html>
```

****
pageL11.html
****

```
<!DOCTYPE html>
<html lang="en">
<head>
<meta charset="utf-8">
<title>Page 11</title>
<style>//CSS goes here</style>
<SCRIPT LANGUAGE="JavaScript">
// javascript functions go here or in body
</SCRIPT>
</head>
<body>
<h3>(JS) Javascript DOD HandBook</h3>
<h4>How to code without coding tools Page 11</h4>
 <center><table><tr><td>     </td><td><button
class="HB"
   onclick="window.location.href = 'site_menu.html';">
      Site Menu
</button></td><td>     </td><td><button class="HB"
   onclick="window.location.href = 'lindex.html';">
      Begin Lessons
   </button></td><td>     </td><td><button class="HB"
```

```
onclick="window.location.href = 'pageL10.html';">
    Last Page
</button></td><td>     </td><td><button class="HB"
onclick="window.location.href = 'pageL12.html';">
    Next Page
</button></td></tr></table></center>
```

(JS) OBJECTS

<p><p><blockquote>

Objects

<blockquote><blockquote><blockquote>
Objects is data stored with one keyword or name but many properties (values)
associated with that name. For instance a car is an object.
A car has many properties associated with it like the manufacture name, model, color, &
how big the engine is.
The key_name = value does that look like a variable? Where as variables are single
instance of name = value; objects are one name: but many values.

There are three ways to declare or create a <b>object</b>.
1st using the objectName={objectName:valueofname1, objectName:valueofname2,
objectName:valueofname3} syntax
like a car={car.name:Dodge, car.model:Charger, car.color:White, car.motor:350Hemi} to
get this car to do something
we will use a <b>method</b> like car.start() or car.brake(). name:Dodge is a key:value
pair of the object car. Value is also
called a <b>property</b>. Thus Dodge:white is the property of the Dodge name.
<i><script>
  car={name:"Dodge", model:"Charger", color:"White", motor:"350Hemi"}
document.write(car.name +" "+ car.model +" "+ car.color +" "+ car.motor +"<br>");
</script></i>
OR to make it easier to read
<i><script>
  car={name:"Dodge", model:"Charger", color:"White", motor:"350Hemi"}
document.write(car.name +" "+ car.model +" "+ car.color +" "+ car.motor +"<br>");

</script></i>

Results below when ran in a script.
<script>
  car={name:"Dodge", model:"Charger", color:"White", motor:"350Hemi"}
document.write(car.name +", "+ car.model +", "+ car.color +", "+ car.motor +"<br>");
</script>

2nd way is declare a variable using the key word "new" Object(); followed by
objectname=value created key:value pair
Like this:
<i><script>
var amCar= new Object();

amCar.name="Ford";
amCar.model="Truck 150";
amCar.color="Blue Tone";
amCar.motor="3.5L Powerboost";
document.write(amCar.name +", "+ amCar.model +", "+ amCar.color +", "+
amCar.motor +"<br>");
</script></i>
The above will yeild this below:
<script>
var amCar= new Object();
amCar.name="Ford";
amCar.model="Truck 150";
amCar.color="Blue Tone";
amCar.motor="3.5L Powerboost";
document.write(amCar.name +", "+ amCar.model +", "+ amCar.color +", "+
amCar.motor +"<br>");
</script>

Third Way is to declare a function name (value1, value2, value3) and use
"<b>this</b>" a keyword to declare
the object names with the value then create a new simpler name for ease of writting it to
the screen. Like this.name=name
Then create a new personnel with id value of Chevy as below.
<i><script>
function cityCar(name, model, color, motor){
this.name=name;
this.model=model;
this.color=color;
this.motor=motor;
}
ccar=new cityCar("Chevy", "Corvette" , "Cherry Red", "6.2L LT2 V8");
document.write(ccar.name +", "+ ccar.model +", "+ ccar.color +", "+ ccar.motor
+"<br>");
</script></i>
Now when we run the script and write to the HTML page you get the following.
<script>
function cityCar(name, model, color, motor){
this.name=name;
this.model=model;
this.color=color;
this.motor=motor;
}
ccar=new cityCar("Chevy", "Corvette" , "Cherry Red", "6.2L LT2 V8");
document.write(ccar.name +", "+ ccar.model +", "+ ccar.color +", "+ ccar.motor +"<br>");
</script>
Advantage to doing it this way you can create many instances of the same information
by changing the input of one line like this:


```
<script>
function cityCar(name, model, color, motor){
this.name=name;
this.model=model;
this.color=color;
this.motor=motor;
}
ccar=new cityCar("Chevy", "Corvette" , "Cherry Red", "6.2L LT2 V8");
document.write(ccar.name +", "+ ccar.model +", "+ ccar.color +", "+ ccar.motor +"<br>");
ccar=new cityCar("Ford", "Truck F150" , "Blue Tone", "3.5L Powerboost");
document.write(ccar.name +", "+ ccar.model +", "+ ccar.color +", "+ ccar.motor +"<br>");
ccar=new cityCar("Dodge", "Charger" , "Pearl White", "350Hemi");
document.write(ccar.name +", "+ ccar.model +", "+ ccar.color +", "+ ccar.motor +"<br>");
</script>
```


The above script displayed:
<script>
function cityCar(name, model, color, motor){
this.name=name;
this.model=model;
this.color=color;
this.motor=motor;
}
ccar=new cityCar("Chevy", "Corvette" , "Cherry Red", "6.2L LT2 V8");
document.write(ccar.name +", "+ ccar.model +", "+ ccar.color +", "+ ccar.motor +"<br>");
ccar=new cityCar("Ford", "Truck F150" , "Blue Tone", "3.5L Powerboost");
document.write(ccar.name +", "+ ccar.model +", "+ ccar.color +", "+ ccar.motor +"<br>");
ccar=new cityCar("Dodge", "Charger" , "Pearl White", "350Hemi");
document.write(ccar.name +", "+ ccar.model +", "+ ccar.color +", "+ ccar.motor +"<br>");
</script>

 Now there are two other ways to create Objects that will be covered in the advanced topics but basically
They are created automatically one is using a constructor and the other is by inheritance. The inheritance is the
Key to DOM the Domain Object Model that creates a Object of any HTML page and so anything displayed can
be accessed and displayed using these properties and methods of Objects. Also Objects can hold Objects, Arrays, and Functions as values
WHEW! Mind blowing like micro world inside of larger world inside a larger world hum is there space alien in the room?

<h3>JavaScript Object Oriented Coding</h3>

Objects hold various information about something as attributes to that something.

Like customer is an object and it can have various attributes that relate to a
customer. Syntax is var customer number ={ attribute 1, attribute 2, and so forth};
Each attribute is separated by a comma and there is a semi-colon at the end.
<script>// Body script tag Javascript Code goes here
document.write("
Begin Object declaration : " + "<br />");
//var cust1 = {name: "John Smith", street: "123 Main Street", city: "Pittsburgh", email:
"jsmith@aol.com", balance: 120.50 };

```
var cust1 = {
name: "John Smith",
street: "123 Main Street",
city: "Pittsburgh",
email: "jsmith@aol.com",
balance: 120.50,


payDownBal: function(amtPaid){
this.balance -= amtPaid;
},
addToBal: function(amtCharged){
this.balance += amtCharged;
}

};
```

document.write("
Writing out the object name and attributes : " + "<br />");

document.write("Customer Name : ", cust1.name, "<br />");
document.write("Customer Street : ", cust1.street, "<br />");
document.write("Customer City : ", cust1.city, "<br />");
document.write("Customer Email : ", cust1.email, "<br />");
document.write("Customer Balance : ", cust1.balance, "<br />");
document.write("
 adding two attributes created via functions: " + "<br />");
document.write("Customer amtPaid : ", cust1.amtPaid, "<br />");
document.write("Customer amtCharged : ", cust1.amtCharged, "<br />");
document.write(" Undefined because no transactions recorded.   " + "<br />");
/*
var amtPaid = 120.5 - 60;
var amtCharged = 60.5 + 20;
document.write("Customer Balance : ", amtPaid, "<br />");
document.write("Customer Balance : ", amtCharged, "<br />");
document.write("
 above manually done not in object " + "<br />");
document.write("
 setting new value in the object " + "<br />");
cust1.amtPaid = 120.5 - 60;
cust1.amtCharged = 60.5 + 20;
document.write("Customer Balance : ", amtPaid, "<br />");
```
```

```
document.write("Customer Balance : ", amtCharged, "<br />");
*/
document.write("Customer moved to 215 State Street change value " + "<br />");
cust1.street = "215 State St.";
document.write("Customer Name : ", cust1.street, "<br />");
document.write("Adding to object country = US " + "<br />");
cust1.country = "US";
document.write("Customer country : ", cust1.country, "<br />");
document.write("adding a state property and attribute " + "<br />");
cust1.state = "PA";
document.write("Customer country : ", cust1.state, "<br />");
document.write("deleting country " + "<br />");
delete cust1.country;
document.write("ReAdding country " + "<br />");
cust1.country = "United States of America";
document.write("Customer country : ", cust1.country, "<br />");
document.write("Properties are the name : attributes are the values " + "<br />");
document.write("Using for - in loop to display all the properties " + "<br />");
for(var prop in cust1){
   if(cust1.hasOwnProperty(prop)){
   document.write(prop, "<br />");
   }
}
document.write("Verify a property of name is in cust1 " + "<br />");
document.write("Name in cust1: ", "name" in cust1, "<br />");
function getInfo(cust){ return cust1.name + " lives at " + cust1.street + ", " + cust1.city +
" , " + cust1.state + " , " + cust1.country + " email: " + cust1.email + " and has a balance
of $" + cust1.balance;}
document.write(getInfo(cust1), "<br>");
document.write("Customer made a payment of 20.50 and then purchased 10.00 more "
+ "<br />");
cust1.payDownBal(20.50);
cust1.addToBal(10.00);
document.write(getInfo(cust1), "<br>");
</script>
<script>
document.write("<br>What if we wanted many customers in the object?" + "<br />");
document.write("We would need to build a generic object using a constructor " + "<br
/>");

document.write("Done by a function Customer\( name, street, city, state, email,
balance\) \{ this.name = name\; this.street = street\; this.city = city\; this.state = state\;
this.email = email\; this.balance = balance\;payDownBal: function(amtPaid){this.balance
-= amtPaid\;}; addToBal: function(amtCharged){this.balance += amtCharged\;}\;\}" +
"<br />");
```

```
document.write("adding generic Customer  " + "<br />");
function Customer(name, street, city, state, email, balance){
this.name = name;
this.street = street;
this.city = city;
this.state = state;
this.email = email;
this.balance = balance;
this.payDownBal = function(amtPaid){
this.balance -= amtPaid;
};
this.addToBal = function(amtCharged){
this.balance += amtCharged;
};
}
document.write("after generic Customer " + "<br />");
document.write("add cust2 " + "<br />");
var cust2 = new Customer("Sally Jones", "234 Oster St.", "Pittsburg", "PA",
"sjones@gmail.com", 0.00);
document.write("adding cust2  " + "<br />");
cust2.addToBal(15.50);
document.write("add new balance " + "<br />");
document.write("Customer Name :  ", cust2.name, "<br />");
function getInfo1(cust){ return cust2.name + " lives at  " + cust2.street + ",  " + cust2.city
+ " , " + cust2.state + " , " + " email: " + cust2.email + " and has a balance of $" +
cust2.balance;}
document.write(getInfo1(cust2), "  2nd getinfo <br>"); //2nd getinfo
var cust3 = new Customer("Thomas Smith", "255 State St.", "Pittsburg", "PA",
"tsmith@aol.com", 120.50);
document.write("adding cust3  " + "<br />");
document.write("Customer Name :  ", cust3.name, "<br />");
function getInfo2(cust){ return cust3.name + " lives at  " + cust3.street + ",  " + cust3.city
+ " , " + cust3.state + " , " + " email: " + cust3.email + " and has a balance of $" +
cust3.balance;}
document.write(getInfo2(cust3), "  3rd getinfo <br>");// 3rd getinfo
document.write(getInfo(cust3), "  first getinfo <br>");// first getinfo

Customer.prototype.isCreditAvail = true;

Customer.prototype.toString = function(){
return this.name + ", " + this.street + ", "+ this.city+ ", "+this.state+ ", "+this.email+ ",
"+this.balance+ ", "+this.isCreditAvail;
};
document.write(cust2.toString());
</script>
<br> Example of inheritance or prototype objects.<br>
```

Demo: Inheritance or using a prototype to create an object.

```
<script>
function Person(firstName, lastName) {
this.FirstName = firstName || "unknown";
this.LastName = lastName || "unknown";
}

Person.prototype.getFullName = function () {
return this.FirstName + " " + this.LastName;
}
function Student(firstName, lastName, schoolName, grade)
{
Person.call(this, firstName, lastName);

this.SchoolName = schoolName || "unknown";
this.Grade = grade || 0;
}
//Student.prototype = Person.prototype;
Student.prototype = new Person();
Student.prototype.constructor = Student;

var std = new Student("James","Bond", "XYZ", 10);

alert(std.getFullName()); // James Bond
alert(std instanceof Student); // true
alert(std instanceof Person); // true
document.write(std.getFullName());
//document.write(Student.firstName);
//document.write(std);
</script>
```

So the script tags show this:
<script>
function Person(firstName, lastName) {
this.FirstName = firstName || "unknown";
this.LastName = lastName || "unknown";
}

Person.prototype.getFullName = function () {
return this.FirstName + " " + this.LastName;
}
function Student(firstName, lastName, schoolName, grade)
{
Person.call(this, firstName, lastName);

this.SchoolName = schoolName || "unknown";
this.Grade = grade || 0;

```
}
//Student.prototype = Person.prototype;<br>
Student.prototype = new Person();<br>
Student.prototype.constructor = Student;<br>

var std = new Student("James","Bond", "XYZ", 10);<br>

alert(std.getFullName()); // James Bond<br>
alert(std instanceof Student); // true<br>
alert(std instanceof Person); // true<br>
document.write(std.getFullName());<br>
//document.write(Student.firstName);<br>
//document.write(std);<br>
&lt;/script&gt;<br>
</blockquote></blockquote></blockquote>

 <center><table><tr><td>     </td><td><button
class="HB"
   onclick="window.location.href = 'site_menu.html';">
     Site Menu
</button></td><td>     </td><td><button class="HB"
   onclick="window.location.href = 'lindex.html';">
     Begin Lessons
  </button></td><td>     </td><td><button class="HB"
   onclick="window.location.href = 'pageL10.html';">
     Last Page
  </button></td><td>     </td><td><button class="HB"
   onclick="window.location.href = 'pageL12.html';">
     Next Page
  </button></td></tr></table></center>

<p style="color:lightgray">
Public Domain copywrite &copy; version 0 - Author retains rights to any additional
versions or editions<br>
Author: Brent Lichfield
</p>
</body>
</html>

******************************

pageL12.html
******************************

<!DOCTYPE html>
<html lang="en">
<head>
<meta charset="utf-8">
```

```html
<title>Page 12</title>
<style>
        .red {
          color: red;
        }
        .purple {
          color: purple;
        }
    </style>
<SCRIPT LANGUAGE="JavaScript">
// javascript functions go here or in body
</SCRIPT>
</head>
<body>
<h3>(JS) Javascript DOD HandBook</h3>
<h4>How to code without coding tools Page 12</h4>
 <center><table><tr><td>     </td><td><button
class="HB"
   onclick="window.location.href = 'site_menu.html';">
     Site Menu
</button></td><td>     </td><td><button class="HB"
   onclick="window.location.href = 'lindex.html';">
     Begin Lessons
   </button></td><td>     </td><td><button class="HB"
   onclick="window.location.href = 'pageL11.html';">
     Last Page
   </button></td><td>     </td><td><button class="HB"
   onclick="window.location.href = 'pageL13.html';">
     Next Page
   </button></td></tr></table></center>
<h3>(JS)DOM GET TAG & ELEMENT SEARCHES</h3>
<blockquote><blockquote><blockquote>
What is the HTML DOM?<br>
The HTML DOM is a standard object model and programming interface for HTML. It
defines:<br>
The HTML elements as <b>objects</b><br>
The <b>properties</b> of all HTML elements<br>
The <b>methods</b> to access all HTML elements<br>
The <b>events</b> for all HTML elements<br><br>
In other words: The HTML DOM is a standard for how to get, change, add, or delete
HTML elements.<br>
HTML DOM methods are <b>actions</b> you can perform (on HTML Elements).<br>
HTML DOM properties are <b>values</b> (of HTML Elements) that you can set or
change.<br>
The DOM Programming Interface<br>
The HTML DOM can be accessed with JavaScript (and with other programming
```

languages).
In the DOM, all HTML elements are defined as <b><i>objects.</i></b>
The programming interface is the properties and methods of each object.
A <b>property </b>is a value that you can <i>get or set</i> (like changing the content of an HTML element).
A <b>method</b> is an action you can do (like <i>add or deleting</i> an HTML element).
document.getElementById("demo").innerHTML = "Hello World!"; The getElementById is a method and the . innerHTML is a property.
This has been how we have displayed text and data to the HTML page. Using a paragraph or divisional tag in HTML.
The innerHTML property can be used to get or change any HTML element, including html and body tags.
Going through all the many methods and things you can do is beyond the scope of this course. <a href=DOM_Methods.html>All the Methods </a>
<p><p><blockquote>

<p id=demo></p>
<p id=demo0></p>
<p id=demo1></p>
<p id=demo2></p>
<p id=demo3></p>
<p id=demo4></p>
<p id=demo5></p>
<p id=demo6></p>
<p id=demo7></p>
<p id=demo8></p>
<p id=demo9></p>
<p id=demo10></p>
<p id=demo11></p>
<p id=demo12></p>
<p id=demo13></p>
<p id=demo14></p>
<p id=demo15></p>
    <h1>querySelectorAll Example</h1>

    <h2>Red Fruits</h2>
    <ul class="red">
      <li>Strawberry</li>
      <li>Raspberry</li>
      <li>Cherry</li>
    </ul>

    <h2>Purple Fruits</h2>
    <ul class="purple">
      <li>Blackberry</li>

```
        <li>Plums</li>
        <li>Grapes</li>
    </ul>

    <script>
        // Selects ALL the <li> elements and adds text to each one
        let listItems = document.querySelectorAll("li");
        for (let i=0; i < listItems.length; i++) {
            listItems[i].innerHTML += " is yummy"
        }

        // Selects the PURPLE <li> elements and make them bold
        let purpleItems = document.querySelectorAll(".purple li");
        for (let i=0; i < purpleItems.length; i++) {
            purpleItems[i].innerHTML += "!!!"
    }

    // Console log the contents of the first items in each list
    // Remember that querySelector returns only the FIRST match
    let firstRed = document.querySelector(".red li");
    //console.log("contents of first red li:", firstRed.innerHTML);
//document.getElementById("demo").innerHTML = firstRed +" is the contents of the red
list";
    let firstPurple = document.querySelector(".purple li");
    //console.log("contents of first purple li:", firstPurple.innerHTML);
//document.getElementById("demo1").innerHTML = firstPurple +" is the contents of the
purple list";
//document.getElementById("demo2").innerHTML = " to view the values within each red
or purple list a 'for \(each\)' item routine is used";
    </script>
 <h1>querySelector Example</h1>
    <p id="description" class="main">
        querySelector's power is exceeded only by it's mystery.
    </p>
    <div id="response">
        It's not that mysterious, querySelector selects elements
        using the same rules as CSS selectors.
    </div>
    <script>
        // selects the <p> using class selector
        let main = document.querySelector(".main");
        console.log(main.innerHTML.trim());
        main.style.color = "blue";

        // Selects the <div> using tag selector
        let response = document.querySelector("div");
```

```
        console.log(response.innerHTML.trim());
        response.style.color = "green";
    </script>
 <h1>innnerHTML Example</h1>

    <h2>Yellow Fruits</h2>
    <ul class="yellow">
      <li>Banana</li>
<li>Kiwi</li>
    </ul>

    <script>
     let ul = document.querySelector(".yellow");
     // console.log(ul.innerHTML.trim());
document.getElementById("demo4").innerHTML = ul.innerHTML.trim() + " selecting
yellow class of unordered list items";

</script>
<br>This login form is going to use the add a event listener to change how the form
works.<br>Remember our example where we used a login to pass information from one
webpage to another? <br>We are going to do that again except we will modify the
output to put the data inside a division HTML element. <br>Then we will search and
select those elements to display what is inside them. <br>
<h3>      Login Here </h3><br>
<form action=loginnext2.html>
  <label for="email">
   Enter your e-mail address:
  </label><br>
  <input type="email" id="email" name="email" />
<br>
  <label for="pwd">
   Enter your Password:
  </label><br>
  <input type="text" id="pwd" name="pass" />
<br>
<br>
     
  <button>Submit</button>
</form>
<script>
const email = document.getElementById("email");
const email = document.getElementById("pwd");

email.addEventListener("input", (event) => {
  if (email.validity.typeMismatch) {
    email.setCustomValidity("I am expecting an e-mail address!");
```

```
    email.reportValidity();
  } else {
    email.setCustomValidity("");
  }
});
</script>


</blockquote></blockquote></blockquote>
 <center><table><tr><td>     </td><td><button
class="HB"
    onclick="window.location.href = 'site_menu.html';">
      Site Menu
</button></td><td>     </td><td><button class="HB"
    onclick="window.location.href = 'lindex.html';">
      Begin Lessons
  </button></td><td>     </td><td><button class="HB"
    onclick="window.location.href = 'pageL11.html';">
      Last Page
    </button></td><td>     </td><td><button class="HB"
    onclick="window.location.href = 'pageL13.html';">
      Next Page
    </button></td></tr></table></center>

<p style="color:lightgray">
Public Domain copywrite &copy; version 0 - Author retains rights to any additional
versions or editions<br>
Author: Brent Lichfield
</p>
</body>
</html>

*******************************
pageL13.html
*******************************
<!DOCTYPE html>
<html lang="en">
<head>
<meta charset="utf-8">
<title>Page 13</title>
<style>//CSS goes here</style>
<SCRIPT LANGUAGE="JavaScript">
// javascript functions go here or in body
</SCRIPT>
</head>
<body style="text-align:center;">
```

(JS) Javascript DOD HandBook

How to code without coding tools Page 13

```
<center><table><tr><td>     </td><td><button
class="HB"
   onclick="window.location.href = 'site_menu.html';">
     Site Menu
</button></td><td>     </td><td><button class="HB"
   onclick="window.location.href = 'lindex.html';">
     Begin Lessons
   </button></td><td>     </td><td><button class="HB"
   onclick="window.location.href = 'pageL12.html';">
     Last Page
   </button></td><td>     </td><td><button class="HB"
   onclick="window.location.href = 'pageL14.html';">
     Next Page
   </button></td></tr></table></center>
```

(JS)QUERYSELECTALL AND QUERYSELECT SEARCHES

```
<blockquote><blockquote><blockquote>

<h1 style="color:#006600" >
GeeksforGeeks
</h1>
<h3> reference https://www.geeksforgeeks.org/jquery-queryselector-vs-
queryselectorall-methods/</h3>
```

This is an illustration of using DOM querySelector() and querySelectorAll(). I have modified it to show how using the querySelector you can
change the color of the text. They do this by putting the text in a division class = test-btn then a function changes the color of the text when you click
on either querySelect button or the querySelectAll button. Note that querySelect only changes the first text field. Where the querySelect changes
all the text fields.

```
<div class="test-btn" style="background-color:#7FFFD4;" >text1</div>
<div class="test-btn" style="background-color:#7FFF00;" >text2</div>
<div class="test-btn"  style="background-color:#8FBC8F;">text3</div>
<div class="test-btn" style="background-color:#7FFF00;">text4</div>

<button onClick="qselector()">
querySelector
</button>

<button onClick="qselectorall()">
querySelectorAll
</button>

<script>
function qselector() {
```

```
document.querySelector(".test-btn")
.style.color = "#DC143C";

}

function qselectorall() {
var x = document
.querySelectorAll(".test-btn");

for (var i = 0; i < x.length; i++) {
x[i].style.color = "#FFFAFA";
}
}
</script>
```

 reference https://www.tutorialstonight.com/queryselector-javascript

Here is another example without a trigger event. The selector looked for .box
anywhere in the class and displayed the first instance with lightgreen background.
.
```
<div class="box">
  <h3>Heading inside the 1st box.</h3>
  <p>This is a paragraph inside the <b>1st box</b>.</p>
</div>
<div class="box">
  <h3>Heading inside the 2nd box.</h3>
  <p>This is a paragraph inside the <b>2nd box</b>.</p>
</div>

<script>
  // selecting element by class
  let element = document.querySelector(".box");

  element.style.background = "lightgreen";
</script>
```

The selector looked for paragraph tag with id that matched id1 and displayed the
first instance with lightgreen background.
.
```
<p id="id1">1st paragraph with id = id1</p>
<p id="id1">2nd paragraph with id = id1 (incorrect use)</p>
<button onclick="getElement1()">Get element</button>

<script>
  function getElement1() {
    // selecting element by its id
    let element = document.querySelector("#id1");

    element.style.background = "lightgreen";
  }
</script>
```


 Here is one that uses a tag name.
<div1>This is a div element.</div>
<div>This is a div element.</div>

<button onclick="getElement2()">Get element by tag name</button>

```
<script>
  function getElement2() {
    let element = document.querySelector("div1");
    element.style.background = "lightgreen";
  }
</script>
```

 Here is one where a title was added and used to make the selection.
<p title="1st item with title">Paragraph with 1st title.</p>
<p title="2nd item with title">Paragraph with 2nd title.</p>
<button onclick="getElement3()">Get element with title attribute</button>

```
<script>
  function getElement3() {
    let element = document.querySelector("[title]");
    element.style.background = "lightgreen";
  }
</script>
```

 Here is example where a anchor tag is used.
<a href="#">link without target attribute</a>
<a href="#" target="_blank">1st link with target attribute</a>
<a href="#" target="_blank">2nd link with target attribute</a>

<button onclick="getElement4()">Get element with target attribute</button>

```
<script>
  function getElement4() {
    let element = document.querySelector("[target]");
    element.style.border = "3px solid black";
    element.style.background = "lightblue";
  }
</script>
```

 Here they match a title
<p title="Some paragraph">My title is "Some paragraph".</p>
<p title="A paragraph">My title is "A paragraph".</p>
<p title="A paragraph">My title is "A paragraph".</p>
<button onclick="getElement5()">Get element with title attribute by value</button>

```
<script>
  function getElement5() {
    let element = document.querySelector('[title="A paragraph"]');
```

```
      element.style.background = "lightgray";
  }
</script>
<br> Here a list is used and they select specific list item<br>
<div id="output">
  <div class="container">
   <ul>
    <li>List item 1</li>
    <li>List item 2</li>
    <li>List item 3</li>
    <li>List item 4</li>
   </ul>
  </div>
  <div class="container">
   <ul>
    <li>List item 1</li>
    <li>List item 2</li>
    <li>List item 3</li>
    <li>List item 4</li>
   </ul>
  </div>
</div>
 <button onclick="getElement6()">Get element</button>

  <script>
   function getElement6() {
    let element = document.querySelector("#output>.container:nth-child(2) ul li:nth-
child(3)");
    element.style.background = "lightgreen";
   }
  </script
<br><br> By a id= number 5 <br>
<h2>Select element by using querySelector.</h2>
  <p>If id or class of an element start with a number then used unicode value to escape
it.</p>
  <div id="4">This is a div element with id=4</div>
  <div id="5">This is a div element with id=5</div>
  <button onclick="getElement7()">Get element</button>

  <script>
   function getElement7() {
    let element = document.querySelector("[id='5']");
    element.style.background = "lightgreen";
   }
  </script>
</blockquote></blockquote></blockquote>
```

```
<center><table><tr><td>     </td><td><button
class="HB"
   onclick="window.location.href = 'site_menu.html';">
      Site Menu
</button></td><td>     </td><td><button class="HB"
   onclick="window.location.href = 'lindex.html';">
      Begin Lessons
   </button></td><td>     </td><td><button class="HB"
   onclick="window.location.href = 'pageL12.html';">
      Last Page
   </button></td><td>     </td><td><button class="HB"
   onclick="window.location.href = 'pageL14.html';">
      Next Page
   </button></td></tr></table></center>

<p style="color:lightgray">
Public Domain copywrite &copy; version 0 - Author retains rights to any additional
versions or editions<br>
Author: Brent Lichfield
</p>
</body>
</html>
```

****
pageL14.html
****

```
<!DOCTYPE HTML>
<HTML lang="en">
<head>
<meta charset="utf-8">
<title>Page 14</title>
<style>//CSS goes here</style>
<SCRIPT LANGUAGE="Javascript">
// Javascript functions go here or in body
</SCRIPT>
</head>
<body>
<h3>(JS) Javascript DOD HandBook</h3>
<h4>How to code without coding tools Page 14</h4><br>
 <center><table><tr><td>     </td><td><button
class="HB"
   onclick="window.location.href = 'site_menu.html';">
      Site Menu
</button></td><td>     </td><td><button class="HB"
   onclick="window.location.href = 'lindex.html';">
```

Begin Lessons
</button></td><td>   </td><td><button class="HB"
onclick="window.location.href = 'pageL13.html';">
Last Page
</button></td><td>   </td><td><button class="HB"
onclick="window.location.href = 'pageL15.html';">
Next Page
</button></td></tr></table>
<p>Lesson Challenge
<blockquote><blockquote><blockquote>
Okay here it is the challenge! You now know the basic tools.
You get to build this one from scratch.
You are a missionary in the deepest part of the jungle assigned to help the mission leader.
Over your radio one of your missionary groups (Peter, Paul & Mary) in the jungle tell you they have found 3
cannibal converts that are traveling with them. The language is a barrier they have been trying to communicate
but all they can get out of the converts is they like the taste of the religion.
<img src="river.jpg" width="200" height="100" alt="River">

They have come to a wide river and
because of flesh eating fish and crockdiles they cannot swim it. They have found one old chopped out tree trunk
canoe but only 2 can go across at a time. They are asking how to get safely across without the converts enjoying
the old religious practice. So you write a small program that will display the proper way for them to get safely
across. Hint: Begin at Bank A if C is for convert > M for missionary on either Bank A or B, dinner is enjoyed by the converts. There is no right
or wrong here just write a program that will get all of them across safely and test it. Like step one 1M+1C go in the canoe
so who gets out on the shore and who takes the canoe back to the other shore. Then what is the next step? And document the steps in your web page so you can relay the information back to your missionary group.
</blockquote></blockquote></blockquote>

<table><tr><td>   </td><td><button
class="HB"
onclick="window.location.href = 'site_menu.html';">
Site Menu
</button></td><td>   </td><td><button class="HB"
onclick="window.location.href = 'lindex.html';">
Begin Lessons
</button></td><td>   </td><td><button class="HB"
onclick="window.location.href = 'pageL13.html';">
Last Page

```
</button></td><td>     </td><td><button class="HB"
onclick="window.location.href = 'pageL15.html';">
    Next Page
    </button></td></tr></table></center>

<p style="color:lightgray">
Public Domain copywrite &copy; version 0 - Author retains rights to any additional
versions or editions<br>
Author: Brent Lichfield
</p>
</body>
</html>
```

```
********************************
pageL15.html
********************************
<!DOCTYPE html>
<html lang="en">
<head>
<meta charset="utf-8">
<title>Page 15</title>
<style>//CSS goes here</style>
<SCRIPT LANGUAGE="JavaScript">
// javascript functions go here or in body
</SCRIPT>
</head>
<body>
<h3>(JS) Javascript DOD HandBook</h3>
<h4>How to code without coding tools Page 15</h4>
 <center><table><tr><td>     </td><td><button
class="HB"
    onclick="window.location.href = 'site_menu.html';">
    Site Menu
</button></td><td>     </td><td><button class="HB"
    onclick="window.location.href = 'lindex.html';">
    Begin Lessons
    </button></td><td>     </td><td><button class="HB"
    onclick="window.location.href = 'pageL14.html';">
    Last Page
    </button></td><td>     </td><td><button class="HB"
    onclick="window.location.href = 'pageL16.html';">
    Next Page
    </button></td></tr></table></center>
<blockquote><blockquote><blockquote>
So How did the challenge go? If you are curious using just "if statements" here is one
solution. <a href=challenge.html> Challenge example</a> Extra points if you used
```

"ifelse-elseif" statements. </blockquote></p>
Author created some "on the fly" or dynamic CSV files using Javascript you might enjoy.
<a href=csv_menu.html> CSV example</a>
Okay DOD hero you now can make CSV files on your own. What if your base got
isolated from internet? Your PC is working and you have this CSV example code.

All the databases that hold your inventory records you cannot reach. Your web
daily log of actions taken to get a DOD machine back online or into the conflict is not

available. Does everyone just sit around till the network comes back up between
bases or the internet? No battles or even deployments do not stop. But you could
keep a log of the actions electronically by creating or using a HTML CSV example. Click
on the link and look for CSV file named AFworklog012422023.csv
You can display or even modify it online save with same name. You can add a new
line(s) for a new day and save it with a new date. This progressive log could be used to

update the large databases when the DOD net returned to service. You could update
commanders on status and return to action estimates. Could enter the
part numbers used on site so they can be restocked when the net returned.
Many of the earliest games were built in JavaScript.
Here are some Applications mostly games available on the internet as searches.
<p><blockquote>

*************************************APPS*************************************
          Calculator <a
href="calculator.html"> Calculator</a>
          Multiply Table <a
href="multiply.html"> mutiply</a>
          Hop Game <a href="hopgame.html">Hip
Hop</a>
          Pong Game <a
href="pong_game.html">Pong </a>
          Space Invaders Game <a
href="space_invaders_game.html">Invader </a>
          Breakout Game <a
href="breakout_game.html">BreakOut</a>
          TO DO LIST <a href="todolist1.html">TO
DO LIST</a>

</p>
</blockquote></blockquote></blockquote>
 <center><table><tr><td>   </td><td><button
class="HB"
   onclick="window.location.href = 'site_menu.html';">
     Site Menu
</button></td><td>   </td><td><button class="HB"
   onclick="window.location.href = 'lindex.html';">
     Begin Lessons
   </button></td><td>   </td><td><button class="HB"

```
onclick="window.location.href = 'pageL14.html';">
    Last Page
</button></td><td>     </td><td><button class="HB"
onclick="window.location.href = 'pageL16.html';">
    Next Page
</button></td></tr></table></center>

<p style="color:lightgray">
Public Domain copywrite &copy; version 0 - Author retains rights to any additional
versions or editions<br>
Author: Brent Lichfield
</p>
</body>
</html>
```

****
pageL16.html
****

```
<!DOCTYPE html>
<html lang="en">
<head>
<meta charset="utf-8">
<title>Page 16</title>
<style>//CSS goes here</style>
<SCRIPT LANGUAGE="JavaScript">
// javascript functions go here or in body
</SCRIPT>
</head>
<body>
<h3>(JS) Javascript DOD HandBook</h3>
<h4>How to code without coding tools Page 16</h4>
 <center><table><tr><td>     </td><td><button
class="HB"
    onclick="window.location.href = 'site_menu.html';">
       Site Menu
</button></td><td>     </td><td><button class="HB"
    onclick="window.location.href = 'lindex.html';">
       Begin Lessons
    </button></td><td>     </td><td><button class="HB"
    onclick="window.location.href = 'pageL15.html';">
       Last Page
    </button></td><td>     </td><td><button class="HB"
    onclick="window.location.href = 'pageL1.html';">
       Next Page
    </button></td></tr></table></center>
<p><blockquote><blockquote><blockquote><center>
```

Congratulations you have completed the DOD-JavaScript-Handbook or How to Code without coding tools.\<br\>
\<img src="celebrate.jpg" alt="Girl in a jacket" width="150" height="250"\>\<br\>
Now select some project you want to do like create one of the games listed on last lesson. Open it with MSNotepad and then save as a\<br\>
different name then improve upon it. OR now you know something about JavaScript you can create Mobile apps with some of the tools\<br\>
available on a cell phone. The Sky is the not the limit but you can do anything given enough code snippets or investigations you make\<br\>
on the internet there is a lot of content out there. Test and try name of the learning game in this industry. As you do you will soon learn\<br\>
that there is a lot more to learn about this language. But learning how to interface other languages with JavaScript is where you become\<br\>
a valued member of the coding world. Good Luck. \<br\>
\</center\>
\</p\>\</blockquote\>\</blockquote\>\</blockquote\>
 \<center\>\<table\>\<tr\>\<td\>   \</td\>\<td\>\<button class="HB"
   onclick="window.location.href = 'site_menu.html';"\>
     Site Menu
\</button\>\</td\>\<td\>   \</td\>\<td\>\<button class="HB"
   onclick="window.location.href = 'lindex.html';"\>
     Begin Lessons
  \</button\>\</td\>\<td\>   \</td\>\<td\>\<button class="HB"
   onclick="window.location.href = 'pageL15.html';"\>
     Last Page
   \</button\>\</td\>\<td\>   \</td\>\<td\>\<button class="HB"
   onclick="window.location.href = 'pageL1.html';"\>
     Next Page
   \</button\>\</td\>\</tr\>\</table\>\</center\>

\<p style="color:lightgray"\>
Public Domain copywrite © version 0 - Author retains rights to any additional versions or editions\<br\>
Author: Brent Lichfield
\</p\>
\</body\>
\</html\>

****
breakout_game.html
****

\<!DOCTYPE html\>
\<html\>
\<head\>

```html
  <meta charset="utf-8" />
  <title>Gamedev Canvas Workshop - lesson 10: finishing up</title>
  <style>* { padding: 0; margin: 0; } canvas { background: #eee; display: block; margin: 0 auto;
}</style>
</head>
<body>

<canvas id="myCanvas" width="480" height="320"></canvas>

<script>
  var canvas = document.getElementById("myCanvas");
  var ctx = canvas.getContext("2d");
  var ballRadius = 10;
  var x = canvas.width/2;
  var y = canvas.height-30;
  var dx = 2;
  var dy = -2;
  var paddleHeight = 10;
  var paddleWidth = 75;
  var paddleX = (canvas.width-paddleWidth)/2;
  var rightPressed = false;
  var leftPressed = false;
  var brickRowCount = 5;
  var brickColumnCount = 3;
  var brickWidth = 75;
  var brickHeight = 20;
  var brickPadding = 10;
  var brickOffsetTop = 30;
  var brickOffsetLeft = 30;
  var score = 0;
  var lives = 3;

  var bricks = [];
  for(var c=0; c<brickColumnCount; c++) {
    bricks[c] = [];
    for(var r=0; r<brickRowCount; r++) {
      bricks[c][r] = { x: 0, y: 0, status: 1 };
    }
  }

  document.addEventListener("keydown", keyDownHandler, false);
  document.addEventListener("keyup", keyUpHandler, false);
  document.addEventListener("mousemove", mouseMoveHandler, false);
```

```javascript
function keyDownHandler(e) {
   if(e.code  == "ArrowRight") {
      rightPressed = true;
   }
   else if(e.code == 'ArrowLeft') {
      leftPressed = true;
   }
}
function keyUpHandler(e) {
   if(e.code == 'ArrowRight') {
      rightPressed = false;
   }
   else if(e.code == 'ArrowLeft') {
      leftPressed = false;
   }
}
function mouseMoveHandler(e) {
   var relativeX = e.clientX - canvas.offsetLeft;
   if(relativeX > 0 && relativeX < canvas.width) {
      paddleX = relativeX - paddleWidth/2;
   }
}
function collisionDetection() {
   for(var c=0; c<brickColumnCount; c++) {
      for(var r=0; r<brickRowCount; r++) {
         var b = bricks[c][r];
         if(b.status == 1) {
            if(x > b.x && x < b.x+brickWidth && y > b.y && y < b.y+brickHeight) {
               dy = -dy;
               b.status = 0;
               score++;
               if(score == brickRowCount*brickColumnCount) {
                  alert("YOU WIN, CONGRATS!");
                  document.location.reload();
               }
            }
         }
      }
   }
}

function drawBall() {
   ctx.beginPath();
   ctx.arc(x, y, ballRadius, 0, Math.PI*2);
```

```javascript
    ctx.fillStyle = "#0095DD";
    ctx.fill();
    ctx.closePath();
}
function drawPaddle() {
    ctx.beginPath();
    ctx.rect(paddleX, canvas.height-paddleHeight, paddleWidth, paddleHeight);
    ctx.fillStyle = "#0095DD";
    ctx.fill();
    ctx.closePath();
}
function drawBricks() {
    for(var c=0; c<brickColumnCount; c++) {
        for(var r=0; r<brickRowCount; r++) {
            if(bricks[c][r].status == 1) {
                var brickX = (r*(brickWidth+brickPadding))+brickOffsetLeft;
                var brickY = (c*(brickHeight+brickPadding))+brickOffsetTop;
                bricks[c][r].x = brickX;
                bricks[c][r].y = brickY;
                ctx.beginPath();
                ctx.rect(brickX, brickY, brickWidth, brickHeight);
                ctx.fillStyle = "#0095DD";
                ctx.fill();
                ctx.closePath();
            }
        }
    }
}
function drawScore() {
    ctx.font = "16px Arial";
    ctx.fillStyle = "#0095DD";
    ctx.fillText("Score: "+score, 8, 20);
}
function drawLives() {
    ctx.font = "16px Arial";
    ctx.fillStyle = "#0095DD";
    ctx.fillText("Lives: "+lives, canvas.width-65, 20);
}

function draw() {
    ctx.clearRect(0, 0, canvas.width, canvas.height);
    drawBricks();
    drawBall();
    drawPaddle();
```

```javascript
        drawScore();
        drawLives();
        collisionDetection();

        if(x + dx > canvas.width-ballRadius || x + dx < ballRadius) {
            dx = -dx;
        }
        if(y + dy < ballRadius) {
            dy = -dy;
        }
        else if(y + dy > canvas.height-ballRadius) {
            if(x > paddleX && x < paddleX + paddleWidth) {
                dy = -dy;
            }
            else {
                lives--;
                if(!lives) {
                    alert("GAME OVER");
                    document.location.reload();
                }
                else {
                    x = canvas.width/2;
                    y = canvas.height-30;
                    dx = 2;
                    dy = -2;
                    paddleX = (canvas.width-paddleWidth)/2;
                }
            }
        }

        if(rightPressed && paddleX < canvas.width-paddleWidth) {
            paddleX += 7;
        }
        else if(leftPressed && paddleX > 0) {
            paddleX -= 7;
        }

        x += dx;
        y += dy;
        requestAnimationFrame(draw);
    }

    draw();
</script>
```

```
</body>
</html>
```

****
calculator.html
****

```html
<html>
<head>
<style>
html,body{
padding:0;
margin:0;
background:whitesmoke;
}

.cont{
position:relative;
width:100%;
padding:0;
margin:0;
text-align:center;
}
.calsi{
width:350px;
padding:0;
margin:100px auto;
text-align:center;
background:#87CEEB;
box-shadow:0px 0px 6px 0px #0006;
}
.calsi h1{
font-size:40px;
font-family:calibri;
font-weight:bold;
color:white;
text-transform:cepitalize;
padding:8px 0px;
text-align:center;
width:100%;
background:#222;
margin:0 auto;
}
```

```css
#inp{
position:relative;
width:100%;
padding:8px 0px;
text-align:center;
font-size:16px;
font-family:arial;
font-weight:normal;
color:#222;
outline:none;
border:none;
background:white;
}
.btns{
position:relative;
width:100%;
padding:10px 0px;
}
.btns button{
border:none;
outline:none;
width:50px;
height:50px;
font-size:30px;
color:#222;
vertical-align:middle;
border-radius:5px;
background:white;
margin:10px 5px;
display:inline-block;
}
button{
border:none;
outline:none;
width:100px;
height:50px;
font-size:20px;
color:#222;
border-radius:5px;
vertical-align:middle;
background:white;
margin:10px 5px;
display:inline-block;
}
```

```html
</style>
</head>
<body>
<div class="cont">
<div class="calsi">
<h1>Calculator</h1>
<input type="text" id="inp" placeholder="Enter Value..." readonly="">
<div class="btns">
<button onclick="AT_add(0)">0</button>
<button onclick="AT_add(1)">1</button>
<button onclick="AT_add(2)">2</button>
<button onclick="AT_add(3)">3</button>
<button onclick="AT_add(4)">4</button>
<button onclick="AT_add(5)">5</button>
<button onclick="AT_add(6)">6</button>
<button onclick="AT_add(7)">7</button>
<button onclick="AT_add(8)">8</button>
<button onclick="AT_add(9)">9</button>
<button onclick="AT_add('+')">+</button>
<button onclick="AT_add('-')">-</button>
<button onclick="AT_add('/')">/</button>
<button onclick="AT_add('*')">*</button>
</div>
<button onclick="exe()">=</button>
<button onclick="cancel()"><⊠</button>
<button onclick="cls()">c</button>
</div>
<script>var val=document.getElementById("inp");

function AT_add(v){
val.value+=v;
}


function cls(){
val.value="";
}

function exe(){
val.value=eval(val.value);
}


function cancel(){
```

```
val.value=val.value.substr(0,val.value.length-1);
}</script>
</body>
</html>
```

```
*******************************
 nada.html
*******************************

*******************************
challenge.html
*******************************
```

```
<!DOCTYPE html>
<html>

<body>
<p id="demo1"></p>
<p id="demo2"></p>
<p id="demo3"></p>
<p id="demo4"></p>
<p id="demo5"></p>
<p id="demo6"></p>


<p><blockquote>
```

You are the help for mission leader.
Over your radio one of your missionary groups (Peter, Paul & Mary) in the jungle tell you they have found 3
cannibal converts that are traveling with them. The language is a barrier they have been trying to communicate
but all they can get out of the converts is they like the taste of the religion. `<br>`
`<center><img src="river.jpg" width="200" height="100" alt="River"></center>`
`<br>`They have come to a wide river and
because of flesh eating fish and crockdiles they cannot swim it. They have found one old chopped out tree trunk
canoe but only 2 can go across at a time. They are asking how to get safely across without the converts enjoying
the old religious practice. So you write a small program that will display the proper way for them to get safely
across. Hint: Begin at Bank A if C is for convert > M for missionary on either Bank A or B, dinner is enjoyed by the converts. . You begin with step one 1M+1C go in the canoe
so who gets out on the shore and who takes the canoe back to the other shore? Then what is the next step? You track the steps in your web page so you can relay the information back to your missionary group.`</blockquote></p>`
Select a canoe option:`<br>`

```html
<ol>
<li><button onclick="numFunction('1')"> One Convert and 1 Missionary added</button></li>
<li><button onclick="numFunction('2')"> Two Converts and NO Missionary added</button></li>
<li><button onclick="numFunction('3')"> Two Missionaries and NO Converts
added</button></li>
<li><button onclick="numFunction('4')"> One Missionary and NO Converts added</button></li>
<li><button onclick="numFunction('5')"> One Convert and NO Missionaries added</button></li>
<li><button onclick="numFunction('6')"> One Missionary and 1 Convert added</button></li>
</ol>
  <script type="text/javascript">
var fc = 3;
var fm = 3;
var sc = 0;
var sm = 0;
var trip = 0;
/*if (trip == 0){
document.getElementById("demo1").innerHTML = ("This is
first trip " + trip + " Begin by loading the canoe");
}*/
//
  function numFunction(num){
//<!--- begin function numFunction
    alert(num);
  canoe = num;
 if ((num!=1) && (trip<1)){
document.write("You did not follow instructions one convert and one missionary must start this
crossing.  <a href=passbuttonvalue_more.html> Click to startover</a>");
}
 if ((trip==1) && (num!=4)){
document.write("You did not make a good choice. Missionaries were eaten notify next of kin and
start over. <a href=passbuttonvalue_more.html> Click to startover</a>");
}
 if ((trip==2) && (num!=2)){
document.write("You did not make a good choice. Missionaries were eaten notify next of kin and
start over. <a href=passbuttonvalue_more.html> Click to startover</a>");
}
 if ((trip==3) && (num!=5)){
document.write("You did not make a good choice. Missionaries were eaten notify next of kin and
start over. <a href=passbuttonvalue_more.html> Click to startover</a>");
}
 if ((trip==4) && (num!=3)){
document.write("You did not make a good choice. Missionaries were eaten notify next of kin and
start over. <a href=passbuttonvalue_more.html> Click to startover</a>");
}
```

```javascript
if ((trip==5) && (num!=6)){
document.write("You did not make a good choice. Missionaries were eaten notify next of kin and start over. <a href=passbuttonvalue_more.html> Click to startover</a>");
}
 if ((trip==6) && (num!=3)){
document.write("You did not make a good choice. Missionaries were eaten notify next of kin and start over. <a href=passbuttonvalue_more.html> Click to startover</a>");
}
 if ((trip==7) && (num!=5)){
document.write("You did not make a good choice. Missionaries were eaten notify next of kin and start over. <a href=passbuttonvalue_more.html> Click to startover</a>");
}
 if ((trip==8) && (num!=2)){
document.write("You did not make a good choice. Missionaries were eaten notify next of kin and start over. <a href=passbuttonvalue_more.html> Click to startover</a>");
}
 if ((trip==9) && (num!=5)){
document.write("You did not make a good choice. Missionaries were eaten notify next of kin and start over. <a href=passbuttonvalue_more.html> Click to startover</a>");
}
 if ((trip==10) && (num!=2)){
document.write("You did not make a good choice. Missionaries were eaten notify next of kin and start over. <a href=passbuttonvalue_more.html> Click to startover</a>");
}
if (num == 1) {
  document.getElementById("demo2").innerHTML = ("The option " + num + " was used to fill the canoe.There is one Convert and one Missionary aboard the canoe.They are paddling...paddling...and paddling to the safe Mission Landing.");
fc --;
fm --;
sc ++;
sm ++;
trip ++;
document.getElementById("demo3").innerHTML = ("This is trip number " + trip + " in reaching safety .There are " +fm + " Missionaries and " +fc + " Converts  at Farside Landing.  There are " +sm + " Missionaries and " +sc + "  Converts on the Mission landing.");
document.getElementById("demo4").innerHTML = ("Select a option for the return trip to Farside landing.");

if (trip==1){
document.getElementById("demo5").innerHTML = ("You have chosen wisely!");
}
return trip;
}
```

```javascript
if (num ==2) {
fc --;
fc --;
sc ++;
sc ++;
trip ++;
  document.getElementById("demo2").innerHTML = ("The option " + num + " was used to fill the
canoe.There is Two Convert and NO Missionaries aboard the canoe.They are
paddling...paddling...and paddling to the safe Mission Landing.");
document.getElementById("demo3").innerHTML = ("This is trip number " + trip + " in reaching
safety .There are " +fm + " missionaries and " +fc + "  converts  at Farside Landing.  There are "
+sm + " Missionaries and " +sc + "  converts on the Mission landing.");
document.getElementById("demo4").innerHTML = ("Select a return trip option to the Farside
Landing");
var rtrip = "Trip was successful " +trip+ "across the river";
document.getElementById("demo6").innerHTML = ("Missionaries are safe"+ rtrip);
//testing if nesting
if (trip==3){
document.getElementById("demo5").innerHTML = ("You have chosen well keep going!");
}


//end of nesting if statements

return trip;
}
if (num ==3) {
fm --;
fm --;
sm ++;
sm ++;
trip ++;
  document.getElementById("demo2").innerHTML = ("The option " + num + " was used to fill the
canoe.There is NO Convert and TWO Missionaries aboard the canoe.They are
paddling...paddling...and paddling to the safe Mission Landing.");
document.getElementById("demo3").innerHTML = ("This is trip number " + trip + " in reaching
safety .There are " +fm + " missionaries and " +fc + "  converts  at Farside Landing. There are "
+sm + " Missionaries and " +sc + "  converts on the Mission landing.");
document.getElementById("demo4").innerHTML = ("Select a return trip  option to the Farside
Landing.");
//testing if nesting
if (trip==5){
document.getElementById("demo5").innerHTML = ("You have used inspiration good for you!");
}
```

```
//end of nesting if statements

return trip;

}

if (num == 4) {
fm ++;
sm --;
trip ++;
   document.getElementById("demo2").innerHTML = ("The option " + num + " was used to fill the
canoe.There is NO Converts and one Missionary aboard the canoe.The Missionary is
paddling...paddling...paddling...paddling...paddling...paddling...and paddling (takes twice as
long) to the  Farside Landing.");
document.getElementById("demo3").innerHTML = ("This is trip number " + trip + " in reaching
safety .There are " + fm  + " Missionaries and " + fc  + "  Converts at Farside Landing. There are
" + sm + " Missionaries and " + sc  + "  Converts on the Mission Landing.");
document.getElementById("demo4").innerHTML = ("Select a new trip to Mission Landing ----
loading of the canoe");

//testing if nesting
if (trip==3){
document.getElementById("demo5").innerHTML = ("After meditation & prayer you have chosen
wisely!");
}


//end of nesting if statements
return trip;
}
if (num ==5) {
fc ++;
sc --;
trip ++;
   document.getElementById("demo2").innerHTML = ("The option " + num + " was used to fill the
canoe.There is 1 Converts and NO Missionary aboard the canoe.The convert is
paddling...paddling...paddling...paddling...paddling...paddling...and paddling to the  Farside
Landing.");
document.getElementById("demo3").innerHTML = ("This is trip number " + trip + " in reaching
safety .There are " + fm  + " missionaries and " + fc  + "  converts at Farside Landing.There are "
+ sm + " missionaries and " + sc  + "  converts on the Mission Landing.");
document.getElementById("demo4").innerHTML = ("Select a new trip to Farside Landing ----
```

```
loading of the canoe");
return trip;
}
if (num == 6){
 document.getElementById("demo2").innerHTML = ("The option " + num + " was used to fill the
canoe.There is one Missionary and one  Convert aboard the canoe.They are
paddling...paddling...and paddling to the Farside Landing.");
sc --;
      sm--;
fm ++;
fc ++;
trip ++;
document.getElementById("demo3").innerHTML = ("This is trip number " + trip + " in reaching
safety .There are " +fm + " missionaries and " +fc + "  converts at Farside Landing.There are "
+sm + " Missionaries and " +sc + "  converts on the Mission landing.");
document.getElementById("demo4").innerHTML = ("Select a new trip to Farside Landing ----
loading of the canoe");
//testing if nesting
if (trip==6){
document.getElementById("demo5").innerHTML = ("You have chosen a good companion for
return trip!");
}


//end of nesting if statements


return trip;
}
//}

//<--- end numFunction
}
 /* if ((num!=1) && (trip<1)){
document.write("You did not follow instructions one convert and one missionary must start this
crossing.  <a href=passbuttonvalue_more.html> Click to startover</a>");
}*/
</script>
<br>
<a href="pageL15.html">Back to Lesson 15</a><br>
</body>
</html>


******************************
```

csv_edit_display_table.html
****

```html
<!DOCTYPE html>
<html>

<head>
   <title>Read CVS File Display as HTML Table</title>
<style>
table, th, td {
border: .1pc solid black;
}
</style>
</head>
<body>
<h3 style="background-color:yellow" align="Center">Read CVS File Display as HTML
Table</h3>
<script type="text/javascript">
   function Upload() {
      var fileUpload = document.getElementById("fileUpload");
      var regex = /^([a-zA-Z0-9\s_\\.\-:])+(.csv|.txt)$/;
      if (regex.test(fileUpload.value.toLowerCase())) {
         if (typeof (FileReader) != "undefined") {
            var reader = new FileReader();
            reader.onload = function (e) {
               var table = document.createElement("table");
               var rows = e.target.result.split("\n");
               for (var i = 0; i < rows.length; i++) {
                  var row = table.insertRow(-1);
                  var cells = rows[i].split(",");
                  for (var j = 0; j < cells.length; j++) {
                     var cell = row.insertCell(-1);
                     cell.innerHTML = cells[j];
                  }
               }
               var dvCSV = document.getElementById("dvCSV");
               dvCSV.innerHTML = "";
               dvCSV.appendChild(table);
            }
            reader.readAsText(fileUpload.files[0]);
         } else {
            alert("This browser does not support HTML5.");
         }
      } else {
         alert("Please upload a valid CSV file.");
```

```
      }
    }
</script>
<input type="file" style="background-color:orange" id="fileUpload" />
<input type="button" style="background-color:lightgreen" id="upload" value="Upload"
onclick="Upload()" />
<hr />
<div id="dvCSV">
</div>
</body>

</html>
```

****
 csv_edit_table_addndelete_rows.html
****

```
<!DOCTYPE html>
<html>
<head>
<title>Table Add or Delete Rows</title>
</head>
<body>
<h1 style="background-color:yellow" align="Center">Add a Row or Delete a Row</h1>
<h2>View HTML table,  use Add new row or delete row </h2>
<h3>Download to CSV by same file name and replace current file with your update.</h3>
<h3>OR keep a history file by placing v1 in the name of the file</h3>
<h3>You will need to open the file with CSV Edit HTML Table and Save to modify text in added
rows.</h3>
  <input type="file" id="myfile" name="myfile" onchange="readfile()">
  <table id="_table" border=1>
</table>
<script>
//Function to read a CSV file
// AND display it as a editable table
function appendJsonToTable(jsonArray){
    const headersHtml = Object.keys(jsonArray[0]).map(h => `<th>${h}</th>`).join('') //if your
table has headers use 1 row (0) as  header
    const tableHtml = jsonArray.map(row => { // create a table array with rows as the elements or
values of the array
      const columns = Object.values(row); // rows as the elements or values of the array next fill
the row array with column values
      const columnsInTable = columns.map(c => `<td contenteditable=true>${c}</td>`).join('')
//contenteditable allows table cell corrections
      return `<tr contenteditable=true>${columnsInTable}</tr>`;
```

```javascript
    }).join('')
    const table = document.getElementById("_table"); // get the elements of the table
    console.log('tableHtml:', tableHtml);
    table.innerHTML = [headersHtml, tableHtml].join('');
}
// take the data string and split it up to extract the actual values into row and column values
function csvToJSON(csvDataString){
    const rowsHeader = csvDataString.split('\r').join('').split('\n')
    const headers = rowsHeader[0].split(',');
    const content = rowsHeader.filter((_,i) => i>0);
    console.log('Headers: ',headers);
    const jsonFormatted = content.map(row => {
        const columns = row.split(',');
        return columns.reduce((p,c, i) => {
            p[headers[i]] = c;
            return p;
        }, {})
    })
    console.log('jsonFormatted:',jsonFormatted);
    // here you have the JSON formatted
    return jsonFormatted;
}
function readfile(e){
    var file = document.getElementById("myfile").files[0];
    const reader = new FileReader();
    reader.addEventListener('load', e => {
        const csvData = e.target.result.toString();
        console.log('CSV Data:', csvData);
        appendJsonToTable(csvToJSON(csvData))
    })
    reader.readAsText(file, 'UTF-8')
}


//Function to convert HTML table into a CSV file and download
//Saving any changes made in a edit
function tableToCSV() {

// Variable to store the final csv data
var csv_data = [];

// Get each row data
var rows = document.getElementsByTagName('tr');
for (var i = 0; i < rows.length; i++) {
```

```javascript
// Get each column data
var cols = rows[i].querySelectorAll('td,th');

// Stores each csv row data
var csvrow = [];
for (var j = 0; j < cols.length; j++) {

// Get the text data of each cell
// of a row and push it to csvrow
csvrow.push(cols[j].innerHTML);
}

// Combine each column value with comma
csv_data.push(csvrow.join(","));
}

// Combine each row data with new line character
csv_data = csv_data.join('\n');

// Call this function to download csv file
downloadCSVFile(csv_data);

}

function downloadCSVFile(csv_data) {

// Create CSV file object and feed
// our csv_data into it
CSVFile = new Blob([csv_data], {
type: "text/csv"
});

// Create to temporary link to initiate
// download process
var temp_link = document.createElement('a');

// Download csv file
temp_link.download = "newfilename.csv";
var url = window.URL.createObjectURL(CSVFile);
temp_link.href = url;

// This link should not be displayed
temp_link.style.display = "none";
document.body.appendChild(temp_link);
```

```javascript
// Automatically click the link to
// trigger download
temp_link.click();
document.body.removeChild(temp_link);
}

/* This method will add a new row */
    function addNewRow(){
        var table = document.getElementById("_table");
        var rowCount = table.rows.length;
        var cellCount = table.rows[0].cells.length;
        var row = table.insertRow(rowCount);
        for(var i =0; i < cellCount; i++){
          var cell = row.insertCell(i);

        if(i < cellCount-1){
            cell.innerHTML='<td contenteditable=true>yadah</td>';
          }else{
  cell.innerHTML='<td contenteditable=true>Yadah</td>';

        }
      }
    }

    /* This method will delete a row */
    function deleteRow(ele){
       var table = document.getElementById('_table');
       var rowCount = table.rows.length;
       if(rowCount <= 1){
          alert("There is no row available to delete!");
          return;
       }
       if(ele){
          //delete specific row
          ele.parentNode.parentNode.remove();
       }else{
          //delete last row
          table.deleteRow(rowCount-1);
       }
    }

</script>
<button type="button"  style="background-color:lightblue" onclick="tableToCSV()">
```

Download CSV to save changes
</button>
<button style="background-color:lightgreen" onclick="addNewRow()">Add New Row</button>
        <button style="background-color:pink" onclick="deleteRow()">Delete Row</button>

<a href="csv_menu.html">Return to CSV Menu</a>
</body>
</html>

****
csv_edit_table_create.html
****

```
<!DOCTYPE html>
<html>
<head>
<meta charset=utf-8 />
<title>Create a table</title>
<style type="text/css">
body {margin: 30px;}
</style>
</head>
<body>
<h3 style="background-color:yellow" align="Center">Create the table first!</h3>
<h3>Input the number of rows and columns you need. Click on Create the table button.</h3>
<h4>     --Next step add the data to the table.</h4>
<h4>     --Ignore and Do Not press "Create the table" button
again.</h4>
<h3>Change the 1st row as headers or column names.</h3>
<h4>     --For data or header data</h4>
<h4>     --Highlight-Select the existing cell data and delete with
keyboard delete key.</h4>
<h3>Input the raw data for each cell of those below row one. </h3>
<h3>Then Save the table giving it a new name. Click "download CSV to save changes button"
only</h3>
<h4>     --Save the new CSV file under a new name in a folder
of your choice.</h4>
<table id="myTable" border="1"  contenteditable="true">
</table><form>
<input type="button" onclick="createTable()" value="Create the table">
</form>
<script>
function createTable()
{
rn = window.prompt("Input number of rows", 1);
cn = window.prompt("Input number of columns",1);
```

```javascript
 for(var r=0;r<parseInt(rn,10);r++)
  {
   var x=document.getElementById('myTable').insertRow(r);
   for(var c=0;c<parseInt(cn,10);c++)
    {
     var y= x.insertCell("<td contenteditable=true>" +c+"</td>");
     y.innerHTML="Row-"+r+" Column-"+c;
//'<td contenteditable=true>${c}</td>'
    }
  }
}
//Function to convert HTML table into a CSV file and download
//Saving any changes made in a edit
function tableToCSV() {

// Variable to store the final csv data
var csv_data = [];

// Get each row data
var rows = document.getElementsByTagName('tr');
for (var i = 0; i < rows.length; i++) {

// Get each column data
var cols = rows[i].querySelectorAll('td,th');

// Stores each csv row data
var csvrow = [];
for (var j = 0; j < cols.length; j++) {

// Get the text data of each cell
// of a row and push it to csvrow
csvrow.push(cols[j].innerHTML);
}

// Combine each column value with comma
csv_data.push(csvrow.join(","));
}

// Combine each row data with new line character
csv_data = csv_data.join('\n');

// Call this function to download csv file
downloadCSVFile(csv_data);
```

```
}
function downloadCSVFile(csv_data) {

// Create CSV file object and feed
// our csv_data into it
CSVFile = new Blob([csv_data], {
type: "text/csv"
});

// Create to temporary link to initiate
// download process
var temp_link = document.createElement('a');

// Download csv file
temp_link.download = "newfilename.csv";
var url = window.URL.createObjectURL(CSVFile);
temp_link.href = url;

// This link should not be displayed
temp_link.style.display = "none";
document.body.appendChild(temp_link);

// Automatically click the link to
// trigger download
temp_link.click();
document.body.removeChild(temp_link);
}
</script>
<button type="button" style="background-color:green"onclick="tableToCSV()">
Download CSV to save changes
</button>
<br><a href="csv_menu.html">Return to CSV Menu</a><br>
</body>
</html>
```

****

csv_edit_table_save_changes.html
****

```
<!DOCTYPE html>
<html>
<head>
<title>Edit Table Cells</title>
</head>
<body>
```

Edit Table Cells save as CSV

Load CSV file, View as HTML table, Cells are Editable, Make changes.

Download to CSV file, overwrite or add version like filenamev1.csv.

```html
  <input type="file" id="myfile" name="myfile" onchange="readfile()">
  <table id="_table" border=1>
</table>
<script>
//Function to read a CSV file
// AND display it as a editable table
function appendJsonToTable(jsonArray){
    const headersHtml = Object.keys(jsonArray[0]).map(h => `<th>${h}</th>`).join('') //if your
table has headers use 1 row (0) as  header
    const tableHtml = jsonArray.map(row => { // create a table array with rows as the elements or
values of the array
        const columns = Object.values(row); // rows as the elements or values of the array next fill
the row array with column values
        const columnsInTable = columns.map(c => `<td contenteditable=true>${c}</td>`).join('')
//contenteditable allows table cell corrections
        return `<tr>${columnsInTable}</tr>`;
    }).join('')
    const table = document.getElementById("_table"); // get the elements of the table
    console.log('tableHtml:', tableHtml);
    table.innerHTML = [headersHtml, tableHtml].join('');
}
// take the data string and split it up to extract the actual values into row and column values
function csvToJSON(csvDataString){
    const rowsHeader = csvDataString.split('\r').join('').split('\n')
    const headers = rowsHeader[0].split(',');
    const content = rowsHeader.filter((_,i) => i>0);
    console.log('Headers: ',headers);
    const jsonFormatted = content.map(row => {
        const columns = row.split(',');
        return columns.reduce((p,c, i) => {
            p[headers[i]] = c;
            return p;
        }, {})
    })
    console.log('jsonFormatted:',jsonFormatted);
    // here you have the JSON formatted
    return jsonFormatted;
}
function readfile(e){
    var file = document.getElementById("myfile").files[0];
    const reader = new FileReader();
```

```javascript
    reader.addEventListener('load', e => {
      const csvData = e.target.result.toString();
      console.log('CSV Data:', csvData);
      appendJsonToTable(csvToJSON(csvData))
    })
    reader.readAsText(file, 'UTF-8')
}

//Function to convert HTML table into a CSV file and download
//Saving any changes made in a edit
function tableToCSV() {

// Variable to store the final csv data
var csv_data = [];

// Get each row data
var rows = document.getElementsByTagName('tr');
for (var i = 0; i < rows.length; i++) {

// Get each column data
var cols = rows[i].querySelectorAll('td,th');

// Stores each csv row data
var csvrow = [];
for (var j = 0; j < cols.length; j++) {

// Get the text data of each cell
// of a row and push it to csvrow
csvrow.push(cols[j].innerHTML);
}

// Combine each column value with comma
csv_data.push(csvrow.join(","));
}

// Combine each row data with new line character
csv_data = csv_data.join('\n');

// Call this function to download csv file
downloadCSVFile(csv_data);

}

function downloadCSVFile(csv_data) {
```

```
// Create CSV file object and feed
// our csv_data into it
CSVFile = new Blob([csv_data], {
type: "text/csv"
});

// Create to temporary link to initiate
// download process
var temp_link = document.createElement('a');

// Download csv file
temp_link.download = "newfilename.csv";
var url = window.URL.createObjectURL(CSVFile);
temp_link.href = url;

// This link should not be displayed
temp_link.style.display = "none";
document.body.appendChild(temp_link);

// Automatically click the link to
// trigger download
temp_link.click();
document.body.removeChild(temp_link);
}
</script>
<button type="button" style="background-color:green"onclick="tableToCSV()">Download as
CSV to save changes</button>
<br><a href="csv_menu.html">Return to CSV Menu</a><br>
</body>
</html>
*******************************

csv_menu.html
*******************************


<!DOCTYPE html>
<html lang="en">
<head>
<meta charset="utf-8">
<title>CSV Menu</title>
<style>//CSS goes here</style>
<SCRIPT LANGUAGE="JavaScript">
// javascript functions go here or in body
</SCRIPT>
```

```
</head>
<body>
<h3 style="background-color:lightgray" align="Center">(JS) Javascript DOD HandBook</h3>
<h4 style="background-color:yellow" align="Center">CSV Menu</h4>
*****************************************CSV_Table_Menu*****************************<br>
<a href="csv_edit_display_table.html">Display as Table Only</a><br>
<a href="csv_edit_table_create.html">Create a new HTML Table</a><br>
<a href="csv_edit_table_addndelete_rows.html">Add a row or Delete a row</a><br>
<a href="csv_edit_table_save_changes.html">CSV Edit HTML Table and Save Changes</a>
<br>
<a href="csv_why.html">Why CSV?</a><br>
<a href="pageL15.html">Back to Lesson 15</a><br>
*****************************************End of Table******************************<br>
<SCRIPT LANGUAGE="JavaScript">
// javascript functions go here or in head
</SCRIPT>
<h5>page 0 </h5>
<p>      Menu Page  <a href="Lsite_menu.html">  Site
Directory</a>     Begining Page <a href="Lindex.html">Start page</a> 
    Previous Page  <a href="pageL7.html">  Last page</a> 
    and Next Page  <a href="pageL9.html">Next page</a></p>
Public Domain copywrite<br>
Author: Brent Lichfield
</body>
</html>


********************************
csv_table_display.html
********************************
<!DOCTYPE html>
<html>

<head>
    <title>Read Text File</title>
<style>
table, th, td {
border: .1pc solid black;
}
</style>
</head>
<body>

<script type="text/javascript">
    function Upload() {
```

```
            var fileUpload = document.getElementById("fileUpload");
            var regex = /^([a-zA-Z0-9\s_\\.\-:])+(.csv|.txt)$/;
            if (regex.test(fileUpload.value.toLowerCase())) {
                if (typeof (FileReader) != "undefined") {
                    var reader = new FileReader();
                    reader.onload = function (e) {
                        var table = document.createElement("table");
                        var rows = e.target.result.split("\n");
                        for (var i = 0; i < rows.length; i++) {
                            var row = table.insertRow(-1);
                            var cells = rows[i].split(",");
                            for (var j = 0; j < cells.length; j++) {
                                var cell = row.insertCell(-1);
                                cell.innerHTML = cells[j];
                            }
                        }
                        var dvCSV = document.getElementById("dvCSV");
                        dvCSV.innerHTML = "";
                        dvCSV.appendChild(table);
                    }
                    reader.readAsText(fileUpload.files[0]);
                } else {
                    alert("This browser does not support HTML5.");
                }
            } else {
                alert("Please upload a valid CSV file.");
            }
        }
</script>
<input type="file" id="fileUpload" />
<input type="button" id="upload" value="Upload" onclick="Upload()" />
<hr />
<div id="dvCSV">
</div>
</body>

</html>

*****************************
csv_why.html
*****************************

<!DOCTYPE html>
<html lang="en">
```

```html
<head>
<meta charset="utf-8">
<title>Why CSV </title>
<style>//CSS goes here</style>
<SCRIPT LANGUAGE="JavaScript">
// javascript functions go here or in body
</SCRIPT>
</head>
<body>
<h3 style="background-color:lightgray" align="Center">(JS) Javascript DOD HandBook</h3>
<h4 style="background-color:yellow" align="Center">Why CSV? </h4>
*******************************************WHY_CSV*******************************<br>
```

When computers were invented they initially were used as gaming machines. But then some one created a text via comma separated values.We know them as
spreadsheets today as a popular term likely coined by Microsoft. But bottom line they could be used to keep inventory, stock prices and mirade of information in
a easy to read format commonly used via paper. When displayed inside a HTML table the data is easy to read and lookup specific values.
Okay DOD Hero what if the power grid went down for weeks at a time or a supernova from the sun wiped out communications in a large portion of the
Pentagon complex and it was going to take weeks or more to get it restored. (Both are a rare occurance but could happen.) Some substations have failed
in the last few years causing area shut downs to electric grids for a week or more. During Civil War a supernova was so strong it wiped out the telegraph stations
batteries and wires melted for several new england states. Even bent the railroad rails in remote spots. So yes it could happen.
So here you sit at a DOD base without access to a internet but with a computer. You have a plane, tank, truck, missile, or what ever war machine and you need
to have it always repaired and alert. You could use the CSV program to create temporary tracking of parts and work performed so when you did access
the webservers that handle that information you could bring them up to date. So this little CSV menu and routines could make you a Hero just because you
Tried to learn coding without any tools.


```html
<a href="csv_menu.html">Back to CSV Menu?</a><br>
<a href="pageL8.html">Back to Lesson 8</a><br>
*******************************************End of Why***********************************<br>
<SCRIPT LANGUAGE="JavaScript">
// javascript functions go here or in head
</SCRIPT>
<h5>page 0 </h5>
<p>      Menu Page  <a href="Lsite_menu.html">  Site
Directory</a>     Begining Page <a href="Lindex.html">Start page</a> 
    Previous Page  <a href="pageL7.html">  Last page</a> 
```

    and Next Page <a href="pageL9.html">Next page</a></p>
Public Domain copywrite
Author: Brent Lichfield
</body>
</html>

****

hopgame.html
****

```html
<!DOCTYPE html>
<html>
<head>
<meta name="viewport" content="width=device-width, initial-scale=1.0"/>
<style>
canvas {
   border:1px solid #d3d3d3;
   background-color: #f1f1f1;
}
</style>
</head>
<body onload="startGame()">
<script>

var myGamePiece;
var myObstacles = [];
var myScore;

function startGame() {
   myGamePiece = new component(30, 30, "red", 10, 120);
   myGamePiece.gravity = 0.05;
   myScore = new component("30px", "Consolas", "black", 280, 40, "text");
   myGameArea.start();
}

var myGameArea = {
   canvas : document.createElement("canvas"),
   start : function() {
      this.canvas.width = 480;
      this.canvas.height = 270;
      this.context = this.canvas.getContext("2d");
      document.body.insertBefore(this.canvas, document.body.childNodes[0]);
      this.frameNo = 0;
      this.interval = setInterval(updateGameArea, 20);
      },
```

```
        clear : function() {
            this.context.clearRect(0, 0, this.canvas.width, this.canvas.height);
        }
    }
}

function component(width, height, color, x, y, type) {
    this.type = type;
    this.score = 0;
    this.width = width;
    this.height = height;
    this.speedX = 0;
    this.speedY = 0;
    this.x = x;
    this.y = y;
    this.gravity = 0;
    this.gravitySpeed = 0;
    this.update = function() {
        ctx = myGameArea.context;
        if (this.type == "text") {
            ctx.font = this.width + " " + this.height;
            ctx.fillStyle = color;
            ctx.fillText(this.text, this.x, this.y);
        } else {
            ctx.fillStyle = color;
            ctx.fillRect(this.x, this.y, this.width, this.height);
        }
    }
    this.newPos = function() {
        this.gravitySpeed += this.gravity;
        this.x += this.speedX;
        this.y += this.speedY + this.gravitySpeed;
        this.hitBottom();
    }
    this.hitBottom = function() {
        var rockbottom = myGameArea.canvas.height - this.height;
        if (this.y > rockbottom) {
            this.y = rockbottom;
            this.gravitySpeed = 0;
        }
    }
    this.crashWith = function(otherobj) {
        var myleft = this.x;
        var myright = this.x + (this.width);
        var mytop = this.y;
```

```javascript
        var mybottom = this.y + (this.height);
        var otherleft = otherobj.x;
        var otherright = otherobj.x + (otherobj.width);
        var othertop = otherobj.y;
        var otherbottom = otherobj.y + (otherobj.height);
        var crash = true;
        if ((mybottom < othertop) || (mytop > otherbottom) || (myright < otherleft) || (myleft >
otherright)) {
            crash = false;
        }
        return crash;
    }
}

function updateGameArea() {
    var x, height, gap, minHeight, maxHeight, minGap, maxGap;
    for (i = 0; i < myObstacles.length; i += 1) {
        if (myGamePiece.crashWith(myObstacles[i])) {
            return;
        }
    }
    myGameArea.clear();
    myGameArea.frameNo += 1;
    if (myGameArea.frameNo == 1 || everyinterval(150)) {
        x = myGameArea.canvas.width;
        minHeight = 20;
        maxHeight = 200;
        height = Math.floor(Math.random()*(maxHeight-minHeight+1)+minHeight);
        minGap = 50;
        maxGap = 200;
        gap = Math.floor(Math.random()*(maxGap-minGap+1)+minGap);
        myObstacles.push(new component(10, height, "green", x, 0));
        myObstacles.push(new component(10, x - height - gap, "green", x, height + gap));
    }
    for (i = 0; i < myObstacles.length; i += 1) {
        myObstacles[i].x += -1;
        myObstacles[i].update();
    }
    myScore.text="SCORE: " + myGameArea.frameNo;
    myScore.update();
    myGamePiece.newPos();
    myGamePiece.update();
}
```

```
function everyinterval(n) {
  if ((myGameArea.frameNo / n) % 1 == 0) {return true;}
  return false;
}

function accelerate(n) {
  myGamePiece.gravity = n;
}
</script>
<br>
<button onmousedown="accelerate(-0.2)"
onmouseup="accelerate(0.05)">ACCELERATE</button>
<p>Use the ACCELERATE button to stay in the air</p>
<p>How long can you stay alive?</p>
</body>
</html>
```

****

html_startup.html
****

```
<!DOCTYPE html>
<html lang="en">
<head>
<meta charset="utf-8">
<title>Basic HTML Page</title>
<style>//CSS goes here</style>
<SCRIPT LANGUAGE="JavaScript">
// javascript functions go here or in body
</SCRIPT>
</head>
<body>
<h3>(JS) Javascript DOD HandBook</h3>
<h4>How to code without coding tools Page 0</h4>
*****************************************NEW Code Below
here***********************************<br>
<br><br>
*****************************************NEW Code ABOVE
here***********************************<br>
<SCRIPT LANGUAGE="JavaScript">
// javascript functions go here or in head
</SCRIPT>
<h5>page 0 </h5>
<p>      Menu Page  <a href="site_menu.html">  Site
Directory</a>     Begining Page <a href="index.html">Start page</a> 
```

    Previous Page <a href="page1.html"> Last page</a>
    and Next Page <a href="page2.html">Next page</a></p>
Public Domain copywrite
Author: Brent Lichfield
</body>
</html>

****

htmlshell.html
****

<!DOCTYPE html>
<html lang="en">
<head>
<meta charset="utf-8">
<title> HTML SHELL Page</title>
<style>//CSS goes here</style>
<SCRIPT LANGUAGE="JavaScript">
// javascript functions go here or in body
</SCRIPT>
</head>
<body>
<h3>(JS) Javascript DOD HandBook</h3>
<h4>HTML Shell of basic HTML commands</h4>
***NEW Code Below
here*************************************
Hello World!
<p>
So as I said in the introduction .htm or .html extention to a file will tell the browser to show a
HTML page. In fact if you save a blank Notepad page as .html with nothing in it will open in a
browser as white blank page. But if you want your user or customer to see something on the
page there are a few necessary commands. First all HTML commands are set within tags. All
html tags have a beginning <tag> and ending tag</tag>. The actual command is an
agreed to keyword command within these tags. There are about 30 commonly used commands
with attributes that can be added to the command. If you wanted to build a bare bones HTML
file the following tagged commands are necessary. And the first start command is the last
ending command this is called nesting commands. HTML interpeter will try to estimate what you
had in mind if you do not follow the nesting but you might get something other than what you
intended.</p> <p> <html>
 <head>
<title> </title>
<style>
</style>
 </head>
<body>

</body>
</html></p>
 <p>Okay so there you have it a basic command set to create a HTML page. If you saved this
(filename).html and then opened in a browser you would get a blank white page.
<html>
 <head>
<title> </title>
<style> </style>
</head>
<body>
Hello World
</body>
</html>
 But if you
added Hello World inside the body tags and refreshed the the page your customer would see

"Hello World" in the top right hand corner.
 The webpage is like blank printer sheet in an old fashion typewriter. There is no default formatting of the page like you get with word processors. You have to give commands to do all any of the things our computer word processor do automatically for you. That is why CSS cascading style sheets are so popular you can do many of those actions for all webpages like define a font, what color is the background other than white, create menus or buttons, or color of the type etc. These basic formating of the page are html commands as well but not applied across pages.
 So let us say we want to add a new line the command <br> and ending tag</br> means break what you are doing and return to the left side of the page on a new line. Now over the years they determined certain ending tags were unnecessary like </br> so generally you can not include it but most commands require begin and ending tags. Or we want to seperate the words on the page with extra spaces add this command & n b s p ; add these together to make a word (take out the spaces /\ between the characters) "/\&/\n/\b/\s/\p/\;"it becomes a non-breaking space or create a tab. Try adding 5 of them for indenting?   or <p> automatically adds new lines infront and at the end of a paragraph   </p> . </p>

<p>So like I said there are about 30 basic commands each with half dozen attributes that can be added to each command changing how it appears on the webpage. I will include a half dozen more commands you will likely see in the javascript lesson for convience but you should study HTML and CSS. W3Schools.com and pagetutor.com are both free and excellent resources.
 If you want to display a image the HTML command is:
<img src="F35.jpg" width="125" height="150" alt="F35">
 <img src="F35.jpg" width="125" height="150" alt="F35"> to copy for your convience.
 To link to a webpage in your directory:
 Template Page <a href="html_startup.html">Template page</a>   Template Page <a href="html_startup.html">Template page</a>
Website page <a href="http://www.yahoo.com/page.html">Yahoo's page</a>   <a href="http://www.yahoo.com/page.html">Yahoo's page</a>
<a href="mailto:scottie@enterprise.com?subject=Beam Me Up!">Email Scottie</a>   <a href="mailto:scottie@enterprise.com?subject=Beam Me Up!">Email Scottie</a>
 </p>

NEW Code ABOVE here********************************
<SCRIPT LANGUAGE="JavaScript">
// javascript functions go here or in head
</SCRIPT>
<h5>HTML Shell </h5>
<p>Begining Page <a href="index.html">Start page</a>   Previous Page <a href="index.html"> Last page</a>   and Next Page <a href="index.html">Next page</a></p>
Public Domain copywrite
Author: Brent Lichfield
</body>
</html>

```
<html>
<body>
```
In JavaScript you cannot use these reserved words as variables, labels, or function names:
```
<table>
<tr><td>abstract</td><td> arguments </td><td>await*</td><td> boolean</td>
<tr><td>break</td><td> byte</td><td> case</td><td> catch</td>
<tr><td>char</td><td> class*</td><td> const</td><td> continue</td>
<tr><td>debugger</td><td> default</td><td> delete</td><td> do</td>
<tr><td>double</td><td> else</td><td> enum*</td><td> eval</td>
<tr><td>export*</td><td> extends*</td><td> false</td><td> final</td>
<tr><td>finally</td><td> float</td><td> for</td><td> function</td>
<tr><td>goto</td><td> if</td><td> implements</td><td> import*</td>
<tr><td>in</td><td> instanceof</td><td> int</td><td> interface</td>
<tr><td>let*</td><td> long</td><td> native</td><td> new</td>
<tr><td>null</td><td> package</td><td> private</td><td> protected</td>
<tr><td>public</td><td> return</td><td> short</td><td> static</td>
<tr><td>super*</td><td> switch</td><td> synchronized</td><td> this</td>
<tr><td><tr><td>throw</td><td> throws</td><td> transient</td><td> true</td>
<tr><td>try</td><td> typeof</td><td> var</td><td> void</td>
<tr><td>volatile</td><td> while</td><td> with</td><td> yield</td>
</table>
```
Words marked with* are new in ECMAScript 5 and 6.
```
<table>
```
JavaScript Objects, Properties, and Methods
You should also avoid using the name of JavaScript built-in objects, properties, and methods:
```
<tr><td>Array</td><td> Date</td><td> eval</td><td> function</td>
<tr><td>hasOwnProperty</td><td> Infinity</td><td> isFinite</td><td> isNaN</td>
<tr><td>isPrototypeOf</td><td> length</td><td> Math</td><td> NaN</td>
<tr><td>name</td><td> Number</td><td> Object</td><td> prototype</td>
<tr><td>String</td><td> toString</td><td> undefined</td><td> valueOf</td>
</table>
```
Java Reserved Words`<br>`
JavaScript is often used together with Java. You should avoid using some Java objects and properties as JavaScript identifiers:`<br>`
getClass`<br>`
java`<br>`
JavaArray `<br>`
javaClass`<br>`
JavaObject`<br>`

JavaPackage

You should also avoid using the name of HTML and Window objects and properties: (DOM objects and properties) & events
<table>
<tr><td>alert</td><td> all</td><td> anchor</td><td> anchors</td>
<tr><td>area</td><td> assign</td><td> blur</td><td> button</td>
<tr><td>checkbox</td><td> clearInterval</td><td>clearTimeout</td><td> clientInformation</td>
<tr><td>close</td><td> closed</td><td> confirm</td><td> constructor
<tr><td>crypto</td><td> decodeURI</td><td> decodeURIComponent</td><td> defaultStatus</td>
<tr><td>document</td><td> element</td><td> elements</td><td> embed</td>
<tr><td>embeds</td><td> encodeURI</td><td> encodeURIComponent</td><td> escape</td>
<tr><td>event</td><td> fileUpload</td><td> focus</td><td> form</td>
<tr><td>forms</td><td> frame</td><td> innerHeight</td><td> innerWidth</td>
<tr><td>layer</td><td> layers</td><td> link</td><td> location</td>
<tr><td>mimeTypes</td><td> navigate</td><td> navigator</td><td> frames</td>
<tr><td>frameRate</td><td> hidden</td><td> history</td><td> image</td>
<tr><td>images</td><td> offscreenBuffering</td><td> open</td><td> opener</td>
<tr><td>option</td><td> outerHeight</td><td> outerWidth</td><td> packages</td>
<tr><td>pageXOffset</td><td> pageYOffset</td><td> parent</td><td> parseFloat</td>
<tr><td>parseInt</td><td> password</td><td> pkcs11</td><td> plugin</td>
<tr><td>prompt</td><td> propertyIsEnum</td><td> radio</td><td> reset</td>
<tr><td>screenX</td><td> screenY</td><td> scroll</td><td> secure</td>
<tr><td>select</td><td> self</td><td> setInterval</td><td>setTimeout</td>
<tr><td>status</td><td> submit</td><td> taint</td><td> text</td>
<tr><td>textarea</td><td> top</td><td> unescape</td><td> untaint</td>
<tr><td>window</td><td> </td><td> </td><td></td>
<tr><td>onblur</td><td> onclick</td><td> onerror</td><td> onfocus</td>
<tr><td>onkeydown</td><td> onkeypress</td><td> onkeyup</td><td> onmouseover</td>
<tr><td>onload</td><td> onmouseup</td><td> onmousedown</td><td> onsubmit</td>
</table>
 Previous Page <a href="pageL3.html"> Back to Lesson 3</a>
</body>
<html>

****
 math.html
****

<html>
  <body>

```html
<script type = "text/javascript">
  <!--
    var a = 33;
    var b = 10;
    var c = "Test";
    var linebreak = "<br />";
document.write(" if then a = 33, b = 10, c = Test");
    document.write(linebreak);

        document.write("a + b = ");
        result = a + b;
        document.write(result);
        document.write(linebreak);

        document.write("a - b = ");
        result = a - b;
        document.write(result);
        document.write(linebreak);

        document.write("a / b = ");
        result = a / b;
        document.write(result);
        document.write(linebreak);

        document.write("a % b = ");
        result = a % b;
        document.write(result);
        document.write(linebreak);

        document.write("a + b + c = ");
        result = a + b + c;
        document.write(result);
        document.write(linebreak);

document.write("a is now " + a);
    document.write(linebreak);
        a = ++a;
        document.write("++a = ");
        result = ++a;
        document.write(result);
        document.write(linebreak);

      document.write("b is now " + b);
    document.write(linebreak);
```

```javascript
        b = --b;
        document.write("--b = ");
        result = --b;
        document.write(result);
        document.write(linebreak);
      //-->
    </script>
<script>
        var a = "33";
        var b = "10";
        var c = "Test";
        var linebreak = "<br />";
document.write(" a = '33' and b = '10' and c = 'test' <br>");
document.write(a + b +" = a and b concatenated");
document.write(linebreak);
document.write(a + b + c +" = a, b, and c concatenated");
    document.write(linebreak);
        var a = 33
        var b = 10;
document.write(" a = 33 and b = 10 and c = 'test' <br>");
document.write("to concatenate the numbers must be converted to strings either directly or
toString method <br> ");
var aa = a.toString();
var bb = b.toString();
document.write("aa is a " + typeof aa +" you can test when you are unsure with a typeof aa
statement<br>");
document.write(" aa = a.toString and bb = b.toString then<br>");
document.write("aa + bb + c + = a, b, and c concatenated <br>");
document.write(aa + bb + c +" = a, b, and c concatenated");
</script>
<br><br>Catenate can sometimes give you an error when you thought you was performing
math. You linked strings instead numbers. <br>
Consider the following code: <br><br>
&lt;script&gt;<br>
document.write("5 + 4 = ", 5 + 4 + "&lt;br /&gt;";// note the comma<br>
document.write("5 + 4 = " + 5 + 4 + "&lt;br /&gt;";// note the + catenate sign<br>
&lt;/script&gt;<br>
<br>
<script>
var num4 = 4;
var num5 = 5;
document.write("5 + 4 = ", 5 + 4 + "<br />");
document.write("5 + 4 = " + 5 + 4 + "<br />");
</script>
```

\
\
Reminder from barebones.\
\<i>\<script\> \
var num1 = 5; \
var num2 = 3;\
var total = num1 + num2;\
document.write (total);\
Addition: var total = num1 + num2; using the + plus sign\
Other math actions you can do is
Subtraction: var total = num1 - num2; using the - negative sign\
Multiplication: var total = num1 * num2; using the * sign\
Division: var total = num1 - num2; using the /divide sign\
Remainder: var total = num1 % num2; using the % percent sign gives remainder of division\
\</script\>\</i>\
   \<script>
var num1 = 5;
var num2 = 3;
//var total = num1 + num2;
//document.write (total);
//Addition: var total = num1 + num2; using the + plus sign
var total = num1 + num2;
document.write (total + "\
");
//Other math actions you can do is Subtraction: var total = num1 - num2; using the - negative
sign
var total = num1 - num2;
document.write (total + "\
");
//Multiplication: var total = num1 * num2; using the * sign
var total = num1 * num2;
document.write (total + "\
");
//Division: var total = num1 / num2; using the / divide sign
var total = num1 / num2;
document.write (total + "\
");
//Remainder: var total = num1 % num2; using the % percent sign gives remainder of division
var total = num1 % num2;
document.write (total + "\
");
\</script>
\
Math has a precedence,multiplication and division before addition or subtraction, what gets
done first can be changed\
 with Parentheses like (a + b) * c this will change the normal
order. \
\
   \<script>
document.write("Addition "+ "\
");
document.write("5 + 4 = " + 5 + 4 + "\
");
document.write("Subraction "+ "\
");
document.write("5 - 4 = " , 5 - 4 + "\
");
document.write("Multiplication "+ "\
");

```
document.write("5 * 4 = ", 5 * 4 + "<br />");
document.write("Division  "+ "<br />");
document.write("5 / 4 = " + 5 / 4  + "<br />");
document.write("Modulus (remainder of division)  "+ "<br />");
document.write("5 % 4 = ", 5 % 4 + "<br />");
</script>
```
Standard way to store numbers in JavaScript

```
<script>
document.write("Max Num =   ", Number.MAX_VALUE+ "<br />");
document.write("Min Num =   ", Number.MIN_VALUE+ "<br />");
document.write("Number are precise only up to 16 places  "+ "<br />");
document.write("Performing precision test adding 0.1000000000000001 to
0.1000000000000001   "+ "<br />");
precisionTest = 0.1000000000000001;
document.write(precisionTest + 0.1000000000000001,"<br />");
document.write("Performing precision test adding one more place beyond 16 places
0.10000000000000001 to 0.10000000000000001   "+ "<br />");
precisionTest = 0.10000000000000001;
document.write(precisionTest + 0.10000000000000001,"<br />");
document.write("Note addition failed and was rounded up common issue in all programing
languages  "+ "<br />");
</script>
<br>
```
Let us say we have a customer that has a yearly balance of 1563.87 and you wanted to give them the chance to pay it off in
monthly installments we can create a math script to do that. By creating a variable var balance = 1563.87 then
document.write("Month Payment : " , (balance/12).toFixed(2), "<br />"); Will provide the equal monthly payment to pay off the balance

```
<script>
var balance = 1563.87;
document.write("Month Payment : " , (balance/12).toFixed(2), "<br />");
document.write("However if we do not fix the rounding to 2 places you get"+ "<br />");
document.write("Month Payment : " , (balance/12), "<br />");
</script>
```
Random Number incrementation: create a random number variable var randNum = 5 then show of increment before or after randNum

```
<script>
var randNum=5;
document.write("randNum++ = " , randNum++, "<br />");
document.write("The incrementation took place after the addition seen above but after it
became randNum is now ", randNum, "<br />");
document.write("++randNum = " , ++randNum, "<br />");
document.write("Decrementation is similar   ", randNum, "<br />");
```

```
document.write("randNum-- = " , randNum--, "<br />");
document.write("The decrementation took place after the subtraction seen above but after it
became randNum is now ", randNum, "<br />");
document.write("--randNum = " , --randNum, "<br />");
</script>
```
Random Number short cut to addition or any other math actions. randNum += 5 etc.

```
<script>
var randNum=5;
document.write("randNum += " , randNum += 5, "<br />");
document.write("randNum -= " , randNum -= 5, "<br />");
document.write("randNum *= " , randNum *= 5, "<br />");
document.write("randNum /= " , randNum /= 5, "<br />");
</script>
```
Order of operations with numbers directly. 3+2*5 is done 2 times 5 then add to three but
parentese change that.

```
<script>
var randNum=5;
document.write("3 + 2 * 5 = " , 3 + 2 * 5, "<br />");
document.write("(3 + 2) * 5 = " , (3 + 2) * 5, "<br />");
</script>
```
List of various built in methods for JavaScript math short list.
In grade school math we could have called these functions but functions is a
reserved word in JavaScript so they call them "methods" instead.

```
<script>
document.write("Math.E = " , Math.E, "<br />");
document.write("Math.PI = " , Math.PI, "<br />");
document.write("Math.abs(-8) = " , Math.abs(-8), "<br />");
document.write("Math.cbrt(1000) = " , Math.cbrt(1000), "<br />");
document.write("Math.ceil(6.45) = " , Math.ceil(6.45), "<br />");
document.write("Math.floor(6.45) = " , Math.floor(6.45), "<br />");
document.write("Math.round(6.45) = " , Math.round(6.45), "<br />");
document.write("Math.log(10) = " , Math.log(10), "<br />");
document.write("Math.log10(10) " , Math.log10(10), "<br />");
document.write("Math.max(10,5) = " , Math.max(10,5), "<br />");
document.write("Math.min(10,5) = " , Math.min(10,5), "<br />");
document.write("Math.pow(4,2) = " , Math.pow(4,2), "<br />");
document.write("Math.sqrt(1000) = " , Math.sqrt(1000), "<br />");
</script>
```
Working with Random numbers like below. Math.floor((Math.random() * 10) +1)

```
<script>
document.write("Random # (1-10) = " , Math.floor((Math.random() * 10) +1), "<br />");
document.write(" Again Random # (1-10) = " , Math.floor((Math.random() * 10) +1), "<br />");
document.write(" Another Random # (1-10) = " , Math.floor((Math.random() * 10) +1), "<br />");
</script>
```

How to convert a string value into a number.

```
<script>
document.write("Converted String: = " , Number("3.14"), "<br />");
document.write(" Convert to an Interger : = " ,parseInt("5"), "<br />");
document.write(" Convert to an Floating number : = " ,parseFloat("5"), "<br />");
</script>
<a href="pageL4.html">  Back to Lesson 4 Math & Operators</a>
  </body>
</html>
```

****
 multiply.html
****

```
<html>
<head>
  <title>Multiplication Table</title>
  <script type="text/javascript">
    var rows = prompt("How many rows for your multiplication table?");
    var cols = prompt("How many columns for your multiplication table?");
    if(rows == "" || rows == null)
    rows = 10;
    if(cols== "" || cols== null)
    cols = 10;
    createTable(rows, cols);
    function createTable(rows, cols)
    {
      var j=1;
      var output = "<table border='1' width='500' cellspacing='0'cellpadding='5'>";
      for(i=1;i<=rows;i++)
      {
    output = output + "<tr>";
        while(j<=cols)
        {
    output = output + "<td>" + i*j + "</td>";
     j = j+1;
     }
     output = output + "</tr>";
     j = 1;
     }
     output = output + "</table>";
     document.write(output);
     }
  </script>
</head>
```

```
<body>
</body>
</html>
```

****
ponggame.html
****

```html
<!DOCTYPE html>
<html lang="en">

<head>
<meta charset="UTF-8">
<meta name ="viewport" content=
"width=device-width, initial-scale=1.0">

<title>PONG GAME</title>

<style>
*{
margin: 0;
padding: 0;
box-sizing: border-box;
}

body {
height: 100vh;
width: 100vw;
background-image: linear-gradient(to top, #ffda77, #ffa45b);
display: flex;
justify-content: center;
align-items: center;
}

.board {
height: 85vh;
width: 80vw;
background-image: linear-gradient(to right, #5c6e91, #839b97);
border-radius: 14px;
}

.ball {
height: 30px;
width: 30px;
border-radius: 50%;
```

```css
position: fixed;
top: calc(50% - 15px);
left: calc(50% - 15px);
}

.ball_effect {
height: 100%;
width: 100%;
border-radius: 100px;
animation: spinBall 0.1s linear infinite;
box-shadow: inset 0 0 18px #fff, inset 6px 0 18px violet,
inset -6px 0 18px #0ff, inset 6px 0 30px violet,
inset -6px 0 30px #0ff, 0 0 18px #fff,
-4px 0 18px violet, 4px 0 18px #0ff;
}

@keyframes spinBall {
100% {
-webkit-transform: rotate(360deg);
transform: rotate(360deg);
}
}

.paddle {
height: 100px;
width: 18px;
border-radius: 50%;
position: fixed;
}

.paddle_1 {
top: calc(7.5vh + 55px);
left: calc(10vw + 30px);
box-shadow: inset 0 0 18px #fff,
inset -6px 0 18px #f3bad6,
inset 6px 0 18px #0ff, inset -6px 0 30px #f3bad6,
inset 6px 0 30px #0ff, 0 0 18px #fff,
4px 0 18px #f3bad6, -4px 0 18px #0ff;
}

.paddle_2 {
top: calc(85vh + 7.5vh - 100px - 55px);
right: calc(10vw + 30px);
box-shadow: inset 0 0 18px #fff,
```

```css
  inset 6px 0 18px #f3bad6,
  inset -6px 0 18px #0ff, inset 6px 0 30px #f3bad6,
  inset -6px 0 30px #0ff,
  0 0 18px #fff, -4px 0 18px #f3bad6, 4px 0 18px #0ff;
}

.player_1_score {
height: 50px;
width: 50px;
color: chartreuse;
position: fixed;
left: 30vw;
margin-top: 30px;
}

.player_2_score {
height: 50px;
width: 50px;
color: chartreuse;
position: fixed;
left: 70vw;
margin-top: 30px;
}

.message {
position: fixed;
/* color: #48426d; */
height: 10vh;
width: 30vw;
color: #c9cbff;
left: 38vw;
margin: 30px auto auto auto;
}
</style>
</head>

<body>
<div class="board">
<div class='ball'>
<div class="ball_effect"></div>
</div>
<div class="paddle_1 paddle"></div>
<div class="paddle_2 paddle"></div>
<h1 class = "player_1_score">0</h1>
```

```html
<h1 class="player_2_score">0</h1>
<h1 class="message">
Press Enter to Play Pong
</h1>
</div>
<script>
let gameState = 'start';
let paddle_1 = document.querySelector('.paddle_1');
let paddle_2 = document.querySelector('.paddle_2');
let board = document.querySelector('.board');
let initial_ball = document.querySelector('.ball');
let ball = document.querySelector('.ball');
let score_1 = document.querySelector('.player_1_score');
let score_2 = document.querySelector('.player_2_score');
let message = document.querySelector('.message');
let paddle_1_coord = paddle_1.getBoundingClientRect();
let paddle_2_coord = paddle_2.getBoundingClientRect();
let initial_ball_coord = ball.getBoundingClientRect();
let ball_coord = initial_ball_coord;
let board_coord = board.getBoundingClientRect();
let paddle_common =
document.querySelector('.paddle').getBoundingClientRect();
let dx = Math.floor(Math.random() * 4) + 3;
let dy = Math.floor(Math.random() * 4) + 3;
let dxd = Math.floor(Math.random() * 2);
let dyd = Math.floor(Math.random() * 2);

document.addEventListener('keydown', (e) => {
if (e.key == 'Enter') {
gameState = gameState == 'start' ? 'play' : 'start';
if (gameState == 'play') {
message.innerHTML = 'Game Started';
message.style.left = 42 + 'vw';
requestAnimationFrame(() => {
dx = Math.floor(Math.random() * 4) + 3;
dy = Math.floor(Math.random() * 4) + 3;
dxd = Math.floor(Math.random() * 2);
dyd = Math.floor(Math.random() * 2);
moveBall(dx, dy, dxd, dyd);
});
}
}
if (gameState == 'play') {
if (e.key == 'w') {
```

```
paddle_1.style.top =
Math.max(
board_coord.top,
paddle_1_coord.top - window.innerHeight * 0.06
) + 'px';
paddle_1_coord = paddle_1.getBoundingClientRect();
}
if (e.key == 's') {
paddle_1.style.top =
Math.min(
board_coord.bottom - paddle_common.height,
paddle_1_coord.top + window.innerHeight * 0.06
) + 'px';
paddle_1_coord = paddle_1.getBoundingClientRect();
}

if (e.key == 'ArrowUp') {
paddle_2.style.top =
Math.max(
board_coord.top,
paddle_2_coord.top - window.innerHeight * 0.1
) + 'px';
paddle_2_coord = paddle_2.getBoundingClientRect();
}
if (e.key == 'ArrowDown') {
paddle_2.style.top =
Math.min(
board_coord.bottom - paddle_common.height,
paddle_2_coord.top + window.innerHeight * 0.1
) + 'px';
paddle_2_coord = paddle_2.getBoundingClientRect();
}
}
});

function moveBall(dx, dy, dxd, dyd) {
if (ball_coord.top <= board_coord.top) {
dyd = 1;
}
if (ball_coord.bottom >= board_coord.bottom) {
dyd = 0;
}
if (
ball_coord.left <= paddle_1_coord.right &&
```

```javascript
      ball_coord.top >= paddle_1_coord.top &&
      ball_coord.bottom <= paddle_1_coord.bottom
    ) {
    dxd = 1;
    dx = Math.floor(Math.random() * 4) + 3;
    dy = Math.floor(Math.random() * 4) + 3;
    }
    if (
      ball_coord.right >= paddle_2_coord.left &&
      ball_coord.top >= paddle_2_coord.top &&
      ball_coord.bottom <= paddle_2_coord.bottom
    ) {
    dxd = 0;
    dx = Math.floor(Math.random() * 4) + 3;
    dy = Math.floor(Math.random() * 4) + 3;
    }
    if (
      ball_coord.left <= board_coord.left ||
      ball_coord.right >= board_coord.right
    ) {
    if (ball_coord.left <= board_coord.left) {
    score_2.innerHTML = +score_2.innerHTML + 1;
    } else {
    score_1.innerHTML = +score_1.innerHTML + 1;
    }
    gameState = 'start';

    ball_coord = initial_ball_coord;
    ball.style = initial_ball.style;
    message.innerHTML = 'Press Enter to Play Pong';
    message.style.left = 38 + 'vw';
    return;
    }
    ball.style.top = ball_coord.top + dy * (dyd == 0 ? -1 : 1) + 'px';
    ball.style.left = ball_coord.left + dx * (dxd == 0 ? -1 : 1) + 'px';
    ball_coord = ball.getBoundingClientRect();
    requestAnimationFrame(() => {
    moveBall(dx, dy, dxd, dyd);
    });
    }
</script>
</body>

</html>
```

```
<!DOCTYPE html>
<html lang="en">
 <head><title>Space Invaders</title></head>
 <body>
  <h1>Space Invaders</h1>
  <!-- Game canvas -->
  <canvas id="canvas" width="800" height="600"></canvas>
  <!-- Javascript game logic -->
  <script>

   // Defines a general class used to specify game objects.
   class GameObject {
     constructor(x, y, width, height, color) {
       // Define the object's position
       this.x = x;
       this.y = y;

       // Define the object's size
       this.width = width;
       this.height = height;

       // Define the object's color
       this.color = color;
     }

     // Draw the object on the canvas
     draw(ctx) {
       ctx.fillStyle = this.color;
       ctx.fillRect(this.x, this.y, this.width, this.height);
     }

     // Update the object's position
     update(dx, dy) {
       this.x += dx;
       this.y += dy;
     }

     // Check if the object is colliding with another object
     collidesWith(obj) {
       return (this.x < obj.x + obj.width
```

```
        && this.x + this.width > obj.x
        && this.y < obj.y + obj.height
        && this.y + this.height > obj.y);
  }
}

// The bullet class defines the properties and behavior of bullets.
class Bullet extends GameObject {
  constructor(x, y, width, height, color, dy) {
    super(x, y, width, height, color);
    // Set the bullet's y direction.
    this.dy = dy;
  }

  update(x, y) {
    this.y += this.dy;
  }
}

// The spaceship class defines the general properties and behavior of the player and
enemies.
  class SpaceShip extends GameObject {
    constructor(x, y, width, height, color, canvasHeight) {
      super(x, y, width, height, color);
      // Set canvas height.
      this.canvasHeight = canvasHeight;
      // Set the spaceship's bullet size.
      this.bulletWidth = 4;
      this.bulletHeight = 8;
      // Set the spaceship's bullet color.
      this.bulletColor = "#ff7800";
      // Bullets fired by the spaceship
      this.bullets = [];
    }

    // Override the draw method to also draw the spaceship's bullets.
    draw(ctx) {
      super.draw(ctx);
      // Draw the spaceship's bullets.
      for (var i = 0; i < this.bullets.length; i++) {
        this.bullets[i].draw(ctx);
        this.bullets[i].update(0, 0);

        // Check if the bullet is out of bounds.
```

```javascript
      if (this.bullets[i].y < 0 || this.bullets[i].y > this.canvasHeight) {
        // Remove the bullet from the array.
        this.bullets.splice(i, 1);
      }
    }
  }

  // A method used to fire bullets from a spaceship
  shoot(dy) {
    this.bullets.push(new Bullet(
      this.x + this.width / 2 - this.bulletWidth / 2,
      this.y - this.bulletHeight,
      this.bulletWidth,
      this.bulletHeight,
      this.bulletColor,
      dy
    ));
  }
}

// The Player class defines the properties and behavior of the player.
class Player extends SpaceShip {
  constructor(x, y, width, height, color, canvasHeight, canvasWidth) {
    super(x, y, width, height, color, canvasHeight);
    this.canvasWidth = canvasWidth;
  }

  // Update the player's position
  update(dx, dy) {
    super.update(dx, dy);

    // Keep the player within the canvas
    if (this.x < 0) {
      this.x = 0;
    } else if (this.x + this.width > this.canvasWidth) {
      this.x = this.canvasWidth - this.width;
    }
  }
}

// The Asteroid class defines the properties and behavior of the asteroids.
class Asteroid {
  constructor(x, y, width, height, color, noParts) {
    // Set an empty array for asteroid parts.
```

```javascript
    this.parts = [];
    // Create the asteroid's parts.
    for (var i = 0; i < noParts; i++) {
      for (var j = 0; j < noParts; j++) {
        this.parts.push(new GameObject(
          x + i * width,
          y + j * height,
          width,
          height,
          color
        ));
      }
    }
  }

  // Draw the asteroid on the canvas.
  draw(ctx) {
    for (var i = 0; i < this.parts.length; i++) {
      this.parts[i].draw(ctx);
    }
  }

  // Check if the asteroid is colliding with another object.
  collidesWith(obj) {
    for (var i = 0; i < this.parts.length; i++) {
      if (this.parts[i].collidesWith(obj)) {
        return true;
      }
    }
    return false;
  }

  // Remove sub object on collide.
  removeOnCollide(obj) {
    for (var i = 0; i < this.parts.length; i++) {
      if (this.parts[i].collidesWith(obj)) {
        this.parts.splice(i, 1);
        break;
      }
    }
  }
}

// Defines an empty object used to specify game properties and behavior.
```

```javascript
var game = {};

// Define canvas and context
game.canvas = document.getElementById('canvas');
game.ctx = game.canvas.getContext('2d');

// Define background color
game.backgroundColor = '#000000';

// Setup asteroids array
game.asteroidsParts = 8;
game.noOfAsteroids = 8;
game.asteroidsSpace = 85;

// Setup enemies
game.enemiesEachLine = 20;
game.enemyLines = 8;
game.enemySpace = 30;
game.enemyFireRate = 1000;
game.enemyFireTimer = 0;
game.enemyDirection = 1;
game.enemyStep = 5;

// Defines a function to handle the game loop
game.update = function() {
  // Draw canvas background
  game.ctx.fillStyle = game.backgroundColor;
  game.ctx.fillRect(0, 0, game.canvas.width, game.canvas.height);

  // Draw player
  game.player.draw(game.ctx);

  // Draw asteroids
  for (var i = 0; i < game.asteroids.length; i++) {
    game.asteroids[i].draw(game.ctx);
  }

  // Draw enemies
  for (var i = 0; i < game.enemies.length; i++) {
    game.enemies[i].draw(game.ctx);
    game.enemies[i].update(game.enemyDirection, 0);
  }

  // Check if the player has destroyed all enemies
```

```javascript
if (game.enemies.length == 0) {
  // Reset the game
  game.restart();
}

// Check if the enemies are out of bounds.
if (game.enemyDirection == 1)
{
  // Find the enemy closest to the right side of the screen
  var closestToRightSideEnemy = game.enemies[0];
  for (var i = 1; i < game.enemies.length; i++) {
    if (game.enemies[i].x > closestToRightSideEnemy.x) {
      closestToRightSideEnemy = game.enemies[i];
    }
  }

  // Check if the enemy closest to the right side of
  // the screen has reached the right side of the screen.
  if (closestToRightSideEnemy.x +
      closestToRightSideEnemy.width > game.canvas.width) {
    // Reverse the direction of the enemies.
    game.enemyDirection = -1;
    // Move the enemies down.
    for (var i = 0; i < game.enemies.length; i++) {
      game.enemies[i].update(0, game.enemyStep);
    }
  }
}
else if (game.enemyDirection == -1)
{
  // Find the enemy closest to the left side of the screen
  var closestToLeftSideEnemy = game.enemies[0];
  for (var i = 1; i < game.enemies.length; i++) {
    if (game.enemies[i].x < closestToLeftSideEnemy.x) {
      closestToLeftSideEnemy = game.enemies[i];
    }
  }

  // Check if the enemy closest to the left side of
  // the screen has reached the left side of the screen.
  if (closestToLeftSideEnemy.x < 0) {
    // Reverse the direction of the enemies.
    game.enemyDirection = 1;
    // Move the enemies down.
```

```
    for (var i = 0; i < game.enemies.length; i++) {
      game.enemies[i].update(0, game.enemyStep);
    }
  }
}

// Enemy fire counter
game.enemyFireTimer += Math.random() * 10;
if (game.enemyFireTimer > game.enemyFireRate) {
  game.enemyFireTimer = 0;
  // Fire enemy bullet
  game.enemies[Math.floor(Math.random() * game.enemies.length)].shoot(5);
}

// Check if player bullet collides with asteroid
for (var i = 0; i < game.player.bullets.length; i++) {
  for (var j = 0; j < game.asteroids.length; j++) {
    if (game.asteroids[j].collidesWith(game.player.bullets[i])) {
      game.asteroids[j].removeOnCollide(game.player.bullets[i]);
      game.player.bullets.splice(i, 1);
      break;
    }
  }
}

// Check if enemy bullet collides with asteroid
for (var i = 0; i < game.enemies.length; i++) {
  for (var j = 0; j < game.enemies[i].bullets.length; j++) {
    for (var k = 0; k < game.asteroids.length; k++) {
      if (game.asteroids[k].collidesWith(game.enemies[i].bullets[j])) {
        game.asteroids[k].removeOnCollide(game.enemies[i].bullets[j]);
        game.enemies[i].bullets.splice(j, 1);
        break;
      }
    }
  }
}

// Check if player bullet collides with enemy
for (var i = 0; i < game.player.bullets.length; i++) {
  for (var j = 0; j < game.enemies.length; j++) {
    if (game.enemies[j].collidesWith(game.player.bullets[i])) {
      game.enemies.splice(j, 1);
      game.player.bullets.splice(i, 1);
```

```javascript
        break;
      }
    }
  }

  // Check if enemy bullet collides with player
  for (var i = 0; i < game.enemies.length; i++) {
    for (var j = 0; j < game.enemies[i].bullets.length; j++) {
      if (game.player.collidesWith(game.enemies[i].bullets[j])) {
        // Reset the game
        game.restart();
        break;
      }
    }
  }

  // Check if an enemy has reached the player's y position.
  for (var i = 0; i < game.enemies.length; i++) {
    if (game.enemies[i].y + game.enemies[i].height > game.player.y) {
      game.restart();
      break;
    }
  }
}

// Defines a function to handle key events
game.keydown = function(e) {
  // If the left arrow key is pressed, move the player left.
  if (e.keyCode == 37 || e.keyCode == 65) {
    game.player.update(-5, 0);
  }
  // If the right arrow key is pressed, move the player right.
  else if (e.keyCode == 39 || e.keyCode == 68) {
    game.player.update(5, 0);
  }
  // If the space bar is pressed, fire a bullet.
  else if (e.keyCode == 32) {
    game.player.shoot(-5);
  }
}

// Defines a function to start the game loop
game.init = function() {
  // Set the game loop
```

```javascript
game.interval = setInterval(game.update, 1000 / 60);

// Setup player
game.player = new Player(
  game.canvas.width / 2 - 50,
  game.canvas.height - 50,
  20,
  20,
  '#0099CC',
  game.canvas.width
);

// Setup asteroids
game.asteroids = [];
for (var i = 0; i < game.noOfAsteroids; i++) {
  game.asteroids.push(new Asteroid(
    game.asteroidsSpace + i * game.asteroidsSpace,
    game.canvas.height - 180,
    5,
    5,
    '#ffffff',
    game.asteroidsParts
  ));
}

// Setup enemies
game.enemies = [];
for (var i = 0; i < game.enemyLines; i++) {
  for (var j = 0; j < game.enemiesEachLine; j++) {
    game.enemies.push(new SpaceShip(
      game.enemySpace + j * game.enemySpace,
      game.enemySpace + i * game.enemySpace,
      20,
      20,
      '#FF0000'
    ));
  }
}
}

// Defines a function to stop the game loop
game.stop = function() {
  clearInterval(game.interval);
}
```

```
    // Defines a function to restart the game
    game.restart = function() {
      game.stop();
      game.init();
    }

    // Start the game on window load
    window.onload = game.init;

    // Detect keydown events
    window.onkeydown = game.keydown;
   </script>
  </body>
</html>
```

```
*******************************
todolist1.html
*******************************
<!DOCTYPE html>

<html>

  <head>

    <title>Task Records</title>

    <style>

body {

   margin: 0;

   min-width: 250px;

   box-sizing: border-box;

}


header {

   background-color: #3682f4;

   padding: 30px 40px;

   color: white;
```

```css
        text-align: center;

    }


label{

    padding: 10px;

    font-size: 26px;

}


ul {

  margin: 0;

  padding: 0;

}


li {

    list-style-type: none;

    padding: 20px;

    margin-inline: 50px;

    margin-block: 30px;

    border-radius: 5px;

    box-shadow: 4px 4px 5px 5px #888888;

    background-color: #3682f4;

    color: white;

    font-size: 20px;

    cursor: pointer;

    width: auto;

    position: relative;
```

```css
}


h2 {

    transition: 0.4s;

    cursor: pointer;

}


h2:hover {

    letter-spacing: 2px;

}


li.checked {

    background: #888;

    color: #fff;

    text-decoration: line-through;

}




.input {

    margin: 10px;

    border: none;

    border-radius: 10px;

    width: 50%;

    padding: 10px;

    font-size: 16px;
```

```css
}

.close {
    position:absolute;
    right: 0;
    top:0;
    margin: 5px;
    padding: 12px 16px 12px 16px;
}

.close:hover {
    color: red;
}

.edit {
    position:absolute;
    right: 0;
    bottom:0;
    margin: 5px;
    padding: 12px 16px 12px 16px;
}

.edit:hover {
    color: green;
}
```

```css
.ct {
    text-align: center;
    justify-content: center;
}


.add {
    background-color: green;
    text-transform: uppercase;
    color:white;
    border-radius: 10px;
    padding: 5px 40px;
    cursor: pointer;

}


.filterList {
    margin-top: 30px;
    position: relative;

}


.filter {
    margin-inline: 20px;
    background-color: rgb(255, 174, 0);
    text-transform: uppercase;
    color:white;
```

```css
      border-radius: 10px;

      padding: 5px 40px;

      cursor: pointer;

}


.scr {

      height: 400px;

      overflow: auto;

}


.info {

      margin-top: 20px;

}


#todos {

      text-align: center;

      justify-content: center;

}


</style>
  </head>
  <body>
    <header class="ct">
      <h2>Task Records</h2>
      <label>Task: </label>
      <input class="input" type="text" id="inp" placeholder="Task..." required>
```

```html
<br>
<label>Priority: </label>
<select class="input" id="priority" required>
    <option value="High A1" selected>High A1</option>
<option value="High A2" selected>High A2</option>
    <option value="High A3" selected>High A3</option>
<option value="High A4" selected>High A4</option>
 <option value="High A5" selected>High A5</option>
    <option value="Medium B1">Medium B1</option>
    <option value="Medium B2">Medium B2</option>
    <option value="Medium B3">Medium B3</option>
    <option value="Medium B4">Medium B4</option>
    <option value="Medium B5">Medium B5</option>
    <option value="Low C1">Low C1</option>
    <option value="Low C2">Low C2</option>
    <option value="Low C3">Low C3</option>
    <option value="Low C4">Low C4</option>
    <option value="Low C5">Low C5</option>
</select>
<br>
<span onclick="addItem()" class="add">Add</span>
<br>
<div class="filterList">
    <label>Filter: </label>
    <span class="filter" id="all" onclick="sortList('all')">ALL</span>
    <span class="filter" id="Low" onclick="sortList('Low')">LOW</span>
```

```html
<span class="filter" id="Medium" onclick="sortList('Medium')">MEDIUM</span>

<span class="filter" id="High" onclick="sortList('High')">HIGH</span>

</div>

<div class="info"><label>Displayed tasks: <span id="inf">0</span></label></div>


</header>

<div class="scr">

<ul id="todos" >

<li>Add a new Task! To complete (cross off) the tasks just click on them. Edit them in the popup window. ABC and 1,2,3 all tasks

do not have same priority. Some are high or urgent meaning must be completed TODAY. Others are Medium due this week,

Low is within the month. We wear many hats professional, parent, spouse, & examplar citizen. Keep things balanced there are

only 24 hours in a  day. Work usually requires 10-14 hours a day, health and sleep requires 7 hours a day. Eat, bathe, hug kids

and spouse. To Keep religious and emotional grounding includes play, service, & worship needs to be scheduled in

or habitual patterns established. Home activities yield X Ten.

</li>


</ul>

</div>



<script>var items = [];//array for to-do-s

var count = 0;//COUNTER FOR ID

var lister = document.querySelector('ul');//checking for completed
```

```javascript
var fltr = "all";//filter default value is 0(all)


addItem = () => {//ADD ITEM FROM FORM FUNCTION
    let todo = document.getElementById("inp").value;
    let priorityGet = document.getElementById("priority").value;


    if(todo && priorityGet){//CHECK IF NOT EMPTY


        var item = {//new object to be added in array
            id: count,
            description: todo,
            priority: priorityGet,
            completed: false
        }


        items.push(item);//push in main array


        document.getElementById("inp").value = "";//CLEAR FIELD


        // console.log(items);


        displayList(items);


        count++;
    }
    else alert("Type something");//no null values
```

```javascript
}


//DISPLAYING ALL THE TO_DO-s
displayList = list => {

    //FIRST, REMOVE ALL PREVIOUS ELEMENTS
    let remove = document.getElementById("todos");
    while (remove.hasChildNodes()) {
        remove.removeChild(remove.firstChild);
    }


    changeInfo(list);


    list.map( elem => {
        let tag = document.createElement("li");//create the li element of the list
        if (elem.completed) tag.setAttribute("class", "checked");
        else tag.setAttribute("class","");
        tag.setAttribute("id",elem.id);


        let text = document.createTextNode(elem.description);//the description of the to-do
        tag.appendChild(text);


        let span = document.createElement("SPAN");//the delete button
        span.setAttribute("class","close");
        span.setAttribute("onclick", `deleteCurrent(${elem.id})`)//using onclick function
        text = document.createTextNode("X");
```

```
        span.appendChild(text);

        tag.appendChild(span);


        let br = document.createElement("hr");//for separation

        tag.appendChild(br);


        text = document.createTextNode(`Priority: ${elem.priority}`);//element priority display

        tag.appendChild(text);


        span = document.createElement("SPAN");//the edit button

        span.setAttribute("class", "edit");

        span.setAttribute("onclick", `editCurrent(${elem.id})`)//using onclick

        text = document.createTextNode("edit");

        span.appendChild(text);

        tag.appendChild(span);


        document.getElementById("todos").appendChild(tag);//append all the info of the list
element

    })

}


//get the current index from the id

currentIndex = id => {

    let checkIndex = el => el.id === id;

    let currentId = items.findIndex(checkIndex);

    return currentId;


}
```

```javascript
//DELETE ITEM FROM LIST WITH FUNCTION ONCLICK
deleteCurrent = id => {

    //delete from array

    items.splice(currentIndex(id), 1);

    if (fltr === "all") displayList(items);

    else sortList(fltr);

}


//EDIT CURRENT TO DO WITH A POPUP
editCurrent = id => {

    let newVal = prompt("Add the new value of this to-do:",items[currentIndex(id)].description);


    if (newVal === null || newVal === ""){//only if not null value

        alert("No new value added. Keeping the old value.");

    }
    else{

        items[currentIndex(id)].description = newVal;

        if(fltr === "all") displayList(items);

        else sortList(fltr);

    }
}


//SORT WITH FILTER TO NEW LIST
sortList = pr => {
```

```javascript
    if(pr != "all"){//if there is a filter applied

        const sorter = items.filter( item => item.priority === pr);

        displayList(sorter);

        fltr = pr;

    }

    else {displayList(items); fltr = "all"}

}


//CHECK/UNCHECK ITEMS WITH EVENT LISTENER

lister.addEventListener('click', check => {

    if (check.target.tagName === 'LI') {

        check.target.classList.toggle('checked');

        items[check.target.id].completed = !items[check.target.id].completed;

        console.log(items[check.target.id]);

    }

}, false);


//change the counter of to-do-s that is displayed

changeInfo = nr => {

    document.getElementById("inf").innerHTML = nr.length;//change innerHTML to display
number

}
</script>
<br>Reference https://github.com/thegreat1411vrishank/priority-based-to-do-list<br>

    </body>

</html>
```
****

varglobal.html

```
********************************
<html>
<body>
<script>
var num1=50; //global variable
var num2=25; //global variable
var num5;
alert(num5 + " is variable num5 value is undefined");
alert(" var is a variable that is Global and can be accessed anywhere inside the script tags.");
function a(){
alert( "global variable named num1 is initialized with number 50");
alert( "global variable named num2 is initialized with number 25");
alert(num1 + " is variable num1 value called inside function a");  // function a obtains the global
variable named value is initialized with number 50
alert(" let and const is a variable that is LOCAL only within the function.");
}
function b(){
//alert( "global variable named value2 is initialized with number 25");
alert(num2 + " is variable num2 value called inside function b");   // function b obtains the global
set  of a variable named value of 25
}
a(); // this is a call for function a to execute the alert box with corresponding value
b();  // this is a call for function b to execute the alert box with corresponding value
function m(){
window.num1 = 100; //declaring global variable by window object
window.num3 = 6*num2; //declaring global variable by window object
let numa = 20;
var numb = 35;
var num5 =5;

window.num5 = 5;
alert(numa + " is variable numa value called inside function m via let keyword");
alert(numb + " is variable numb value called inside function m via var keyword");
alert(num1 + " is variable num1 value changed and called inside function m via a window.value
object");

}

window.num5 = 5;
alert(num1 + " is variable num1 value Outside in function m");
alert( " variable numa is undeclared Outside in function m trying to call it will cause program to
stop");
//alert(numb +  " variable numb is undeclared Outside in function m trying to call it will cause
program to stop");
```

```javascript
alert(num5 + " is variable num5 declared outside the function m value is  shown Outside in
function as a new value to num5");

function
n(){
alert(window.num3 + " inside function m created global num3 to 6 times num2 & displayed in
this alert");//accessing global variable from other function
}
// alert(num3 + " is variable num3 value Outside in function m created in m via window.value
object "); this failed to produce a global variable num3

m(); // this is a call for function m to execute the alert box with corresponding value added by
window.value
n(); // this is a call for function m to execute the alert box with corresponding value added by
window.value
var num1=75;
function d(){
alert(window.num1 + " changed var num1 inside the function d");//accessing global variable
using window value
}
d();
alert(num1 + " is variable num1 value changed and called outside function d");
alert(num1 + " is variable num1 value is now 75 but if we return to top of the script & refresh the
page num1 should be 50");

</script>
```

Global variables remain useable through out the script tags. Functions however are local
variables and as such they are temporary and will not be passed to a global area or scope for
use. You can however create a global variable and initialize that variable inside a function and
or show it to the screen as document.write or DOM print. Changing the variable inside a function
changes the original variable initialization while inside the function. DOD basically allows only
"strict" plain vanilla javascript. Many of the advanced features from 2006 onward is disabled.
 Previous Page <a href="pageL3.html"> Back to Lesson 3</a>
</body>
</html>

****
****
Copy-> Paste and Save as a .csv file. The document type (Save as type) needs to change to
ALL Files before adding the name and saving the file in the folder. Default document type is .txt
and will be added automatically unless you specify ALL Files.
****

AFworklog012422023.csv

```
*******************************
AC-Id,Symptoms,Analysis,Repair-Actions,Parts used,Status
ID992,popped rivets left wing,Corrosion stress,Wing removed and rivets replaced,Rivets and paint,Onsite repairs - 30 days
HL543,nose gear sag,leaking nose seal,Remove nose wheel and replace,Nose seal replaced,Onsite repairs - 30 days
AB907,Gatlin gun raddle,Mounting broke,replace broke mounting,Ordered #14378 part 1-17-2023,Awaiting part - 60 days
BR911,fuel transfer wine,Air getting into fuel,Replace seals to piping,Metal shop re-building seals &amp; lines ,Awaiting lines - 45 days
HC892,flaps down AC slides left,mounting not correct,Reset the mounting shear pins and test,Shear pins,Onsite repairs - 30 days
*******************************

data.csv
*******************************

car name,miles/gallon,cylinders,displacement,horsepower,weight,acceleration,model year,origin
"chevrolet chevelle malibu",18,8,307,130,3504,12,70,1
"buick skylark 320",15,8,350,165,3693,11.5,70,1
"plymouth satellite",18,8,318,150,3436,11,70,1
*******************************

 employee.csv
*******************************

name,role,country
Sarene,Help Desk Operator,Thailand
Olvan,Nurse Practicioner,China
Janos,Cost Accountant,China
Dolph,Assistant Manager,China
Ariela,Database Administrator I,Azerbaijan
Lane,Environmental Tech,Indonesia
Griselda,Senior Quality Engineer,Portugal
Manda,Physical Therapy Assistant,Brazil
Leslie,Information Systems Manager,Japan
Aleen,Cost Accountant,Canada
*******************************

goods.csv
*******************************

Canned Good, Use by Date, Quantity, Minimum needed
Green Beans, Sep 2030,28,24
Spam, Dec 2028, 12, 20
Corn, Oct 2029, 22, 24
Evap Milk, Jan 2024, 12, 24
Peas, Aug 2027, 20, 24
Fruit Cocktail, Jul 2029, 12, 24
Dried Mash Potatoes, Jul 2045, 5, 10
```

Oatmeal milled, Jun 2046, 5, 12
Sugar canned, May 2035, 5, 12
****

homevideo.csv
****

Video Name,Genre,year,key actor or actress
The 10 commandments,Religious,1965,Charlton Heston

****
persons.csv
****

Name,Profession,Age,Hobby
Cristiano,Hacker,24,Travelling, Sky-diving
Jenifer,Photographer,22,Cooking
Simon,Travelling-guide,35,Dancing, Gardening
Cristiano Ronaldo,Footballer,29,Singing
****

phones.csv
****

userId,userCell,userHome
Susan Rose,801-586-0390,801-771-0390
Tiny Timothy,385-435-2341,801-435-1234
****

workers.csv
****

name,role,country
Sarene,Help Desk Operator,Thailand
Olvan,Nurse Practicioner,US
Janos,Cost Accountant,UK
Dolph,Assistant Manager,Mexico
Ariela,Database Administrator I,Philippines
Lane,Environmental Tech,Indonesia
Griselda,Senior Quality Engineer,Portugal
Manda,Physical Therapy Assistant,Brazil
Leslie,Information Systems Manager,Japan
Aleen,Cost Accountant,Canada